5-8-12

Rod Colón

Shilpa,

Own Your
Career,

Introduces the
Empowering Today's
Professionals Network

Rod Colón

Win the Race
for 21st Century
Jobs

Put CEO Power into Your Job Search
and Your Career

with
Chip Hartman

etp *Network*
Running the Business of "ME"

Published by ETP Network Press
Address information requests or inquiries to
ruth@etpnetwork.com or check the ETP Network website
at **www.etpnetwork.com**.

Front and back cover design by Chip Hartman
Text design by Richard Laurent
Editing by Cheryl Jefferson
Production Management by Ruth Harenchar

Second Edition
ISBN **978-0-615-31568-3**

Running the Business of "ME"

Table of Contents

Foreword

by ETP Network Chief Operations Officer
Carl E. Reid

Preface by ETP Network Founder an
Chief Executive Officer, Rod Colón

Chapter 1
Welcome to the ETP Network

Chapter 2
The Machinery:
Build, Track and Maintain Your Network

Chapter 3
The Mentality: Run Your Career As A Business

Chapter 4
The Magnet: Your Value Proposition

Chapter 5
The Methodology: The 7-Step Job Search Methodology

Chapter 6
The Hidden Job Market

Chapter 7
The Interview and Negotiations

Chapter 8
Once You've Landed

Chapter 9
Putting It All Together and Troubleshooting

Chapter 10
Social Networking: Be A Part of It!

Chapter 11
The Awesome Power of Attitude and Behavior

Chapter 12
Break Away From The Pack

Foreword

Every so often someone crosses your path who becomes a lightning rod that changes your life forever. For me, the turning point was meeting Mr. Rod Colón back in January of 1999. While exploring consulting opportunities, a friend suggested I contact Rod to discuss tactics and strategies. As I recall, he had no leads to share with me at that time; nevertheless I walked away from that meeting with a strange and inspiring thought: Whatever Rod Colón was involved in, I wanted to be a part of it. He had brilliant business insights, an animated, uplifting and thoroughly engaging personality, and what appeared to be a sixth sense about how to help people find jobs.

Fast forward to the year 2001. Rod had begun sending out an email career management newsletter to all of his contacts in transition. Although the economy was unstable and there were extensive job losses, he never missed a week in sending out job posts, inspiring articles, and a refreshingly positive outlook on life. That newsletter became a beacon of hope for many weary job seekers, some of whom were on the brink of giving up altogether.

After a flurry of e-mail exchanges over the years, Rod suggested we meet in person to discuss areas of mutual interest and what shook out of that meeting was truly extraordinary: we discovered that we shared the "business ownership" view of career management, that is, career professionals can only survive if they adopt the model of running their careers as a profitable business.

For me, my involvement with Rod's emerging network began as a member of his newly formed organization, the Empowering Today's Professionals Network. From active member to event leader to program manager, I am fortunate today, five years later, to be the Chief Operations Officer of the ETP Network.

For those who genuinely want to stay competitive in today's volatile job market, Win the Race for 21st Century Jobs is a must read for career professionals, entrepreneurs and smart business leaders. Rod has laid out a master strategy for not only staying in the race but pushing ever closer to the front of the pack.

If it's possible for lightning to strike twice, it happened again when I met co-author Chip Hartman, himself a Rod Colón convert and active ETP Network leader. As the ETP Network's Editor-in-Chief, Chip's authorship of Win the Race for 21st Century Jobs is a powerful endorsement of Rod's career management philosophy and his unique job search methodology.

I hope you will be as inspired by this book as Chip and I have been in having our lives touched by this truly remarkable and gifted man.

Carl E. Reid

Carl E. Reid, CSI
Chief Operations Officer, Empowering Today's Professionals Network
Speaker, Author,chnologist and Business Career Coach
www.CarlEReid.com

Preface

When friends learn that I've written a book about my networking organization, the **ETP Network** (*Empowering Today's Professionals*) *they often ask, "Rod ... There are at least 15,000 books out there about networking. Why write another one? For one thing, this isn't just another book about networking. This book is about a bold new approach to finding jobs, client and business opportunities — as well as performing complete career makeovers. It's about helping business professionals win the race for 21st century jobs.*

The second reason for writing this book — a far more compelling reason in my view — is that **it was the right thing to do and now was the right time to do it.**

Many people out there are in pain. Their financial situations are dire. They have lost their jobs, their life savings and in many cases, their self-respect while chasing around looking for a new position.

It's that "chasing around" part that started to bother me many years ago. Long before today's economic turmoil started creeping toward critical mass, it became obvious to me that far too many people were conducting their job searches in an illogical and self-defeating way. They were lured into the easy, deceptive world of Internet job boards where hunting for a job simply meant finding an interesting opening, uploading a resume and cover letter, clicking a few buttons, then waiting for a response.

I used to imagine job seekers sitting by the phone, waiting for that special call from a key decision-maker telling them that, yes, they'd been chosen for an interview and to please make all the necessary preparations.

But the folly of this approach is that the job board, at best, is nothing more than a piece of software. It can not engage in meaningful two-way communication with humans. Without a human-to-human "networking" component in the equation, how can anyone expect to get meaningful results?

This is the connectionless void in which so many people have spent thousands of hours toiling their lives away in the false hope that a database somewhere in cyberspace would electronically ride to their rescue, find them a job, reinstate the flow of money into their households, and make things right with the world again.

How much more wrong could they have possibly been?

Hello. My name is Rod Colón. I am the Founder and CEO of the ETP Network. ETP stands for "Empowering Today's Professionals" and that is exactly what we do in this unique organization. We teach people how to take control of their careers in the same way a Chief Executive Officer directs all critical operations of a large corporation.

The key difference separating the ETP Network from every other networking organization can be traced back to something that happened to me in the 1990s when I worked as an executive recruiter and hiring manager at J. P. Morgan.

The position gave me an unobstructed, 20/20 view of both sides of the interviewer's desk. I learned a great deal about the mistakes made by candidates applying for jobs **as well as** the techniques and strategies used by hiring managers to screen those very same candidates.

I knew what hiring managers were looking for — the best talent for the companies they represented. After all, everyone knew these managers earned their salaries by correctly and consistently choosing the best talent to meet the needs of their employers.

It's easy to see why hiring managers continue to live by these same stringent standards. In today's high-pressure business environment, these individuals still have the strongest leverage in the entire job search process — **and they use it!**

I wanted to find a way for job seekers like you to reduce that leverage by applying some leverage of your own. I concluded that you needed to grasp, master and integrate four critical skills:

1. Exceptionally effective networking
2. Thinking and acting like the CEO of a large corporation
3. Developing a bulletproof value proposition to make you as attractive as possible to decision-makers, and
4. Expertise at following a precisely-targeted 7-step job search methodology that leads you directly to an interview.

In order to do this, I realized it would be necessary to set up a highly specialized **networking and career management training organization.**

That's what the ETP Network is and that's what differentiates it from almost all networking organizations where the emphasis is on making introductions, giving 30-second elevator speeches, exchanging business cards, then calling it a night.

Today, you will be hard pressed to find another networking organization that matches what the ETP Network does.

Our signature benefit to members is the 7-step job search methodology, unavailable anywhere else, that provides a clear and logical path for moving from "in-transition" to "employed."

You are most welcome to join us on your job search journey. We are here to teach you, coach you, guide you, and inspire you. We are **not** here to do the heavy lifting for you — *that is your job entirely.* While you manage your job search as the CEO of ME, Inc., we will be here to support you in winning the race for 21st century jobs.

But please be careful: Contrary to what you may hear elsewhere, *there is absolutely no free ride to your next position.* Although Internet job boards may be useful for gathering information, that's where their practical value ends.

To really make progress, you need a team that's already been on the journey you're taking now, a willingness to commit to some very hard work, and the mental toughness to see the program through to completion.

The ETP Network *is* that team. I hope you will join us.

Rod Colón

Founder and CEO, The ETP Network
www.etpnetwork.com

For Mom and Dad

Introduction

The Job Search: It's Your Decision

There are two ways to conduct a job search in the 21st century. One has a dismal track record. The other one, a newcomer to the job search landscape, has been specifically engineered for both short- and long-term success.

Whichever method you choose is entirely up to you. You can stay with the traditional method if you don't mind extended periods of frustration and emotional distress. Or you can take charge of your own career with a bold new system that:

- places full accountability for success on your own shoulders

- demands the best you have to offer, nothing less; and

- requires you to have **mental toughness** and a **positive mental attitude.**

This book describes that bold new system and provides a plan for winning the race for 21st century jobs.

The Other Side of the SUBMIT Button

Let's set the stage. The so-called "traditional" approach to the job search goes something like this:

First, you tidy up your resume, slap a cover letter on top, then check the Internet job boards for a position that looks like a good fit. Sometimes there's a form you need to fill out with some personal information. As a final step, you'll probably need to attach your documents then click the SUBMIT button. Easy, quick, and effective.

Well, not quite. Easy? – yes. Quick? – yes. Effective? – *No way!*

Did you ever stop to think about what actually happens on the *other side* of that SUBMIT button? Who actually *gets* your resume anyhow? Are they dutifully passing your paperwork up the line to an appropriate decision-maker for review? Or are they making paper airplanes out of it? And by the way, how would you ever know?

One thing is certain: Since *you* don't know *them* and they don't know *you*, it's a safe bet that they will have little interest in helping you. Why should they? You mean nothing to them. You're just another name on another resume. I'll bet that your plumber has more name recognition with you than you do with the nameless, faceless people on the other side of the SUBMIT button.

As you can probably guess, this type of job search leads to extended periods of waiting, worrying and wondering. In most cases, you end up with woefully little information regarding status and updates. Your patience wears thin while your blood pressure climbs. You get no response, no feedback, no status of any kind. You're left completely in the dark. It's as if your resume has just been sucked into some enormous black hole in space. And for all practical purposes, it has.

The Black Hole

Don't get me wrong about those people on the other side of the SUBMIT button. I'm sure they are very nice, friendly, and perform their work honestly and ethically. They may belong to the same civic organizations, read the same books, shop at the same stores, and browse the same web sites as you. But nothing changes the fact that they don't know you and you don't know them ... *are you beginning to see the problem?* **There is no human-to-human interaction here. You are conducting your job search in a connectionless environment.**

The people who handle Internet-based resume submissions are part of a nebulous region of the business universe that I call **The Black Hole.** When you send your resume and cover letter into The Black Hole, it almost always ends up in exactly the same place: **nowhere.**

There's another disturbing aspect to the Black Hole. When we solve problems, human nature typically drives us to find the shortest distance between two points. Call me a skeptic, but I'm highly suspicious of an approach that requires so little effort to achieve as formidable a goal as landing a new job. In my mind, this is a perfect example of the **GIGO Principle:** Garbage In ... Garbage Out. Hardly any **effort in** ... hardly any **value out.** If you ask me, that's a pretty flimsy model on which to pin any hopes for securing an income for you and your family. While it's true that some individuals will luck out and find a job using The Black Hole, the majority will not. The majority will endure disappointment, frustration, and heartache because they will wait endlessly for a response that — when you really stop to think about it — has no rational reason for ever being sent.

Over the past few years, I've collected some disturbing statistics about job seekers who rely on The Black Hole approach:

- **85%** get absolutely no response – at least not from the client.

- **10%** get a generic response – "Don't call me, I'll call you."

- **3%** get a "discount store special" – companies looking to undercut value.

- **2%** get a client telephone screen, i.e., some type of contact with a client.

Let's put things in perspective. Most people use The Black Hole for two reasons:

1. It's easy; and
2. There are no other options.

I won't deny the seductive simplicity of Reason # 1. But I have a lot to say about Reason # 2 – *a whole lot.* In fact Reason # 2 is the very reason I wrote this book.

So if you're thinking about staying with a job search methodology simply because it's easy and convenient, just remember: It's "Click and Wooooosh!" — off your resume goes — *off into The Black Hole* — **probably forever!**

A Seismic Shift for the 21st Century Job Search

Up until a few years ago, The Black Hole was the only game in town. Today, that's no longer true. In 2004, I started engineering a whole new job search system for professionals who wanted to manage their careers in the same way a CEO manages a company.

The system is logical, precise, and driven by CEO-style business logic. It leverages the power of **advocates** — people who will help you get connected to decision-makers or contacts who know those decision-makers — within a company that interests you. It requires you to develop a powerful **value proposition** which, if designed correctly, will just about require any sensible decision-maker to grant you an interview.

The system is starting to pick up traction on blogs, networking and job search web sites, and local newspapers, but the message is **really** starting to gain attention on social networking sites like *LinkedIn, Facebook* and *Twitter.*

There's a good reason for this: **It gets results.** In the past six months alone, our "landing rate" has almost tripled.

There are four key components to my job search system:

Users must:

1. Develop their **networking skills** in order to form relationships based on mutual trust and reciprocity
2. Adopt a **CEO mentality** in running their careers as a business
3. Craft a compelling **value proposition** that will attract the attention of any decision-maker
4. Follow a precise **7-Step Job Search Methodology** for carrying out their search.

The work will be demanding. There are no shortcuts or guarantees. Your commitment to the program is purely binary: **You're either in it to win it, or you're not in it at all. Let's get started.**

The ETP Network Job Search System

The **ETP Network Job Search System** consists of four core components:

Sequence	Component	Function	Description
1	Networking	The Machinery	Make solid connections and build a warm, trusted network; then maintain it with care.
2	CEO of ME, Inc.	The Mindset	Adopt the CEO of ME, Inc. mind set to run your career as a business.
3	Value Proposition	The Magnet	Design a powerful, compelling value proposition that leads to an interview everytime.
4	7-Step Job Search	The Methodology	Learn, master, then execute Rod Colón's 7-Step Job Search Methodology

ETP Network members who learn and absorb this system *significantly* shrink the time between the initial discovery of a suitable job description and the call for an interview.

To cite just one example of how this is accomplished, I teach members how to build a powerful case for their candidacy with bulletproof relevance and memorable impact.

I also train them to build **value propositions** that are so compelling that they practically require decision-makers to keep an extra interview slot open; after all, how can they refuse to interview someone who meets **or even exceeds** the published requirements?

In adopting this methodology for the job search, ETP Network members begin to view their role in the process as gradually shifting from an "employee mind set" (i.e., dependence on traditional corporate hierarchies) to a "CEO of ME, Inc." mind-set (i.e., an independent business owner), complete with all necessary adjustments to develop a **positive mental attitude** and a continuous supply of **mental toughness.**

Success or Failure is a Matter of Choice

I designed this program so that individuals with the highest level of commitment will achieve the greatest success. This is precisely what The Black Hole does **not** offer.

That said, not everyone is comfortable with my system.

I've seen this situation many times in the past five years: Members join the organization with the best of intentions, step themselves through some orientation material, get off to a reasonably good start — then pull back when they realize that the full burden of "working the program" rests on *their* shoulders alone.

But most ETP Network members find the experience challenging, energizing, and inspirational. They like the idea that their next job (or client) is right around the corner. They like the feeling of being in control of all decisions and actively managing different aspects of their career "enterprise" to achieve success. And they especially like the freedom that comes from knowing they are no longer shackled to The Black Hole.

The Situation Then and the Situation Now
One message I want to be especially clear about is this: In the late 20th century (generally the early 1990s), the employer/employee model under which most of us labored convinced us that we would always have a position as long as we worked hard and performed at or above expectations.

That model no longer exists. Now it's up to individual "CEOs" to direct the business functions of their own careers, e.g., "R & D" (networking and market intelligence), "Sales & Marketing" (resume and interviewing), etc... in order to secure a viable niche in the business landscape of the 21st century.

For better or worse, *you are and will be engaged in an uncomfortably tight race for employment survival in the decades to come.* This book lays out the rules for that race and asserts that your only real chance of winning is to boldly leave old-style job search thinking in the dust.

I firmly believe that the **ETP Network Job Search System** is the best single defense against any extended periods of transition and the needless suffering endured by you and your family as a result.

The "Paul Revere" of Networking Organizations

In his book The World is Flat, (Copyright 2005, Farrar, Straus, & Giroux), *New York Times* columnist Thomas Friedman presents a view of the future in which evolving technologies will level the playing field for business owners worldwide. Traditional corporate hierarchies will likely be replaced by highly specialized online communities sharing similar business interests.

According to Friedman, to survive in this ever-flattening world, individuals must diversify their skills so that they remain viable competitors across many different careers. Those who do, those who attain a level of specialization that cannot be outsourced are, he claims, "untouchable." So if you want job security, join their ranks. *Become an "untouchable" now.*

And if you don't? The fallout from such dramatic technological change may mean that those who haven't kept pace will lose the race for 21st century jobs.

The ETP Network is staking out territory in this new world to keep its members informed, educated, inspired, and prepared for sweeping change by teaching the *CEO*

of ME, Inc. mind-set. Individuals who have learned to manage their careers as a business will be well-positioned to deal with whatever comes their way. Those who don't may well find themselves swallowed up in the connectionless void of The Black Hole.

This applies to some networking groups, too. Through this book, I will be sending a wake-up call to those organizations that still believe networking is about tossing indiviuals into a room where they listen to each other's elevator pitches, exchange business cards, and then call it a day.

Networking is much, much more than that. Networking is learning about the most effective ways to connect with others. It's about building solid, trusted relationships from those connections then nurturing those relationships. In fact, networking is the insurance policy you take out to secure a place for yourself in the relationship-based global economy of the future.

Finally, networking is just *good sound business.* Through effective networking you build one of the greatest assets to ensure your place as a viable contender in the race for 21st century jobs: *business intelligence.*

As the CEO of ME, Inc., you will use that intelligence to run your career as a business and the one activity you must never stop is networking. It's the machinery that drives your CEO of ME, Inc. business. That shouldn't come as a big surprise; after all, no effective CEO could stay in business long if he or she stopped making contacts — without them, your days as a CEO of ME, Inc. or anything else **would be** numbered.

Some Important Points to Keep in Mind ...

Just in case you're thinking, "Gee, I'll read this book, go home and follow all the directions, and get an interview tomorrow", brace yourself for some unsettling news:

1. *I cannot guarantee you a job just because you read this book, join the ETP Network or follow my program.* No one can guarantee you a job. What I **can** offer you is a road map to get you much, much closer to an interview and "getting your foot in the door" **compared with anything** The Black Hole could ever offer. My program increases the ***probability for success*** in your job search.

2. *No one can make this program work for you except you.* I will carry out the instructional heavy lifting with the capable assistance of my leadership team. The membership will do its part to support you and help you to succeed.

3. *Attitude is everything.* If you tend to rely on excuses to get by, the ETP Network will **not** be a good fit for you. If you continually whine and complain, the ETP Network will **not** be a good fit for you. If you are impatient, self-absorbed, or believe that you are somehow entitled to all of the good things in life without having to work for them, you should return this book for an exchange or refund.

4. *A word about networking.* This is not a book **about** networking; it's a book about **the ETP Network** Job Search System that **uses** networking as one of its four

cornerstones. If you are new to networking, there are some great books available to provide the basics. A terrific starting point, in my view, is the best-seller <u>Never Eat Alone</u>, (Copyright 2005, Currency-Doubleday) by Keith Ferrazzi. Mr. Ferrazzi uses a common sense approach to networking that carries a clear and powerful message for those in the race for 21st century jobs.

5. *Read the whole book and read the chapters in their proper sequence.* While some books are written so that readers can jump around and find what interests them based on chapter titles, this is not one of them. The true message of this book can only be processed if you read it cover-to-cover.

6. *Things you should know about Rod the person.* If you and I will be developing a relationship someday (which is my hope and expectation), there are some things I'd like you to know and understand about me:

- I don't coddle. I've never done it and never will. I believe coddling damages a person's sense of self-worth. I believe in coaching people to bring out the very best they have within. If you expect me to be a "yes man" just to make you feel good, you're joining the wrong organization.

- I believe in the appropriate use of "tough love",i.e., requiring individuals to accept responsibility for the consequences of their own decisions. Don't confuse this with being brutish, rude, or disrespectful because I am none of those things. I simply feel that in many cases, some individuals have lapsed into complacency with their job search and an occasional dose of cold, hard reality is appropriate.

- I don't back down from confrontations. You may find that a bit unsettling, especially in the beginning. Don't misinterpret what I'm doing: I'm trying to expose the raw nerve of a prob-lem that looks to me like something you seem unwilling to face and fix.

- I am honest and straightforward with everyone. My goals are set clearly in my mind and I believe the program I have developed will help many individuals if they are willing to make the commitment to follow it without deviation.

Saving the Best for Last

Once you learn, test, and master the ETP Network Job Search System, you'll greatly reduce the risk of suffering and the misery that comes as a result of extended "dry spells" between jobs. **The jobs are out there.** *(Not only that, there are "hidden jobs" out there if you know where to look for them, and I've reserved an entire chapter to explore this fascinating corner of the business world.)*

This program ensures that you remain plugged into the networking machinery that leads to your next job because it requires you to accept full responsibility for keeping your network nourished. Even when you get your next job, you will still be using these principles since you'll now be in a "business-to-business" relationship with your employer instead of an "employee-employer" relationship.

This system will work — if you "work the system."

How This Book is Organized

Chapter 1
Welcome to the ETP Network

The ETP Network (Empowering Today's Professionals) was established specifically to help individuals in transition find jobs. Find out the how's, who's, what's and why's of this amazing organization and its Founder and CEO, Mr. Rod Colón.

Chapter 2
TheMachinery:
Build, Track and Maintain Your Network

The modern day job search is built on the machinery of networking. If you're new to networking, this chapter gives you the basics, beginning with the art of small talk all the way up to the development of a warm, trusted network.

Chapter 3
The Mentality: Run Your Career as a Business

Once you start the network machinery running, the next step is training yourself to think of your job search as a business with you as its CEO. All of the decisions affecting your job search begin and end with you and you will learn the fine art of taking responsibility for them.

Chapter 4
The Magnet: Your Value Proposition

As you begin to identify opportunities that look like a good fit for you, you'll learn how to develop a solid value proposition (the job description, a "targeted resume" and a special cover letter called a "T-Letter"). This is the magnet that will attract employers to you.

Chapter 5
The Methodology:
The 7-Step Job Search Methodology

The centerpiece of the ETP Network is a precisely-engineered 7-Step Job Search Methodology. You will locate perfectly matched opportunities, find and leverage advocates within the company using polished networking skills, and submit your value proposition.

Chapter 6
The Hidden Job Market

Many individuals who are looking for jobs are unaware that there is a Hidden Job Market! The Hidden Job Market consists of positions that have not been advertised and positions that don't yet exist — because the employer has not yet realized the need for the position!

Chapter 7
The Interview and Negotiations

Discover the secrets that will make you shine during an interview. Yes, there is significant preparation; but this list of tips has been assembled from years of experience as a **decision-maker***. These are the tips and techniques that provide the inside track to effective interviews.*

Chapter 8
Once You've Landed

The time to put new energy into your networking activities is when you're offered a new position. Ironically, this is exactly when many people abandon their networks only to discover their mistake later when they need help and their networks have withered.

Chapter 9
Putting It All Together and Troubleshooting

Networking, the CEO of ME, Inc., the Value Proposition, and the 7-Step Job Search Methodology: You learned them as separate pieces; now it's time to put them all together so that the whole program makes sense. This is where we'll do some extensive trouble-shooting, too.

Chapter 10
Social Networking: Be a Part of It!

The explosion of social media and social networking web sites like LinkedIn, Twitter and Facebook demands that those in the race for 21st century jobs remain well-connected. Networking makes my system work; social networking sites are places to make new connections!

Chapter 11
The Awesome Power of Attitude and Behavior

*If there is any true obstacle to overcome in learning the **ETP Network** Job Search **System**, it's the battle that must be fought in your own mind to embrace and adopt all its components. Getting your attitude and behavior "in line" is the key step in helping you to win the race.*

Chapter 12
Break Away From the Pack

Everyone has unique talents and abilities, but not everyone knows how to draw them out and leverage them for success in the business world. In Chapter 12, you'll discover how you can differentiate yourself from the competition and break away from the pack. Most importantly, you'll get a sense of just where the "finish line" in the race for 21st century jobs really is!

Beyond ME, Inc.

Just when you thought the story was over there's a whole new begin-ning — and it's got "business success" written all over it! After establishing yourself as a winner in the race for 21st century jobs, find out what it takes to leverage your victory into profitable business ventures.

Acknowledgements

Index

Rod Colón — Profile

Chapter 1

Welcome to the ETP Network

1.1 Run Your Career as a Business

Who are the most important people in your life? The most popular answer to that question is: "My family." For most of us, "family" represents those individuals who believe in us and trust us to provide them with the necessities of life.

I now ask you to begin thinking of your family as your **Personal Board of Directors.** These are the people to whom you have the greatest responsibility and who will benefit the most from your successful job search. They are also the individuals who endure hardship if your search is unproductive and there's no other source of income. Put another way, your Personal Board of Directors deserves to have you working at nothing less than peak performance during your search.

That's why learning to detach from the grip of The Black Hole is so essential. While The Black Hole is a no-brainer to use, that personal comfort level comes with a steep price tag: no acknowledgement of resumes and cover letters, no status updates via e-mail or phone calls, and no invitations for interviews ... just to name a few. And getting miserable results like that does **nothing** to support your Personal Board of Directors.

I don't know about you, but if I'm in a job search and I have a choice between an approach that's easy to use but lightweight on results or a methodology that requires me to work hard but produces consistently favorable results, I'll go with **the more demanding option** every time. Why? There's simply far too much at stake.

To get started and overcome the addictive force of The Black Hole and Black Hole-style thinking, I require all new members of the ETP Network to commit whole-heartedly to the following paradigm:

> *Each individual will promote himself or herself to the position of CEO of ME, Inc. and make a conscious decision to run his or her own career as a business.*

What's the benefit? By segmenting your job search into "branches" or "divisions" (e.g., Research & Development, Sales & Marketing, etc.) that correlate with a traditional corporate structure, you can train yourself to develop two key attributes that are missing from the Black Hole: **personal accountability** and **workload distribution.** Together they are an unbeatable combination compared to piling all tasks into one overstuffed filing cabinet in your brain — which often leads to chaos and the need to assign blame when the load becomes unmanageable.

This ME, Inc. paradigm is also the centerpiece for my *7-Step Job Search Methodology.* The beauty of the program is that new ETP Network members learn how to integrate their business divisions into a meaningful, end-to-end process that's sensible, manageable, and measurable; that's right — you can develop metrics that will tell you if you're making progress and help you pinpoint any disconnects.

About the ETP Network
(Empowering Today's Professionals)
The ETP Network has engineered an entirely new type of job search built on four key interrelated goals. Members will:

1. Develop and refine all networking skills
2. Adopt the CEO of ME, Inc. mind-set
3. Create powerful and compelling value propositions to attract potential employers
4. Use a precise, step-by-step approach that leverages the connecting power of advocates to help you "network your way" to key people in the hiring process

The power of this system is its ability to reduce the time between the next suitable opportunity and the call for an interview. It will help you connect the dots — but only if you work it properly. And that is a key point: *first you need to learn it, then you need to "work it."*

I'd like to welcome you to this incredible organization. We are all about *power networking, power business ownership, power value propositions,* and an incredible new power job search methodology all rolled up into one.

1.2 We Are Networking Professionals

My friends often tease me, saying: "Rod, you're always networking. Why not give it a rest?" They might as well say, "Rod, you're always breathing. Why not give it a rest?" My answer is the same for both questions: "I can't."

For me, networking is all about interacting with people no matter who they are, where they are, or what they're doing. It could be members of my family, neighbors, members of the PTA, or the UPS driver. I don't care. I gravitate to people because they fascinate me. I love them. They charge me up and give meaning to my life. Everyone has a story to tell, and I love hearing those stories.

Of course that's the practical, everyday, "fun" side of networking. I need to make sure you understand the *business imperative* of networking, too.

That's why I now tell you this: If you decide not to pursue my job search methodology geared for 21st century jobs, be absolutely sure you read the following passage before making the decision final:

> Relationships are the new "capital" of the 21st century and as such, will have a much greater impact on growth in almost every business sector of the economy. If you opt out of networking, you are taking yourself out of the career landscape for a long time to come. This is one of the reasons why the ETP Network exists: It's not JUST about the job search, it's about becoming masters of networking with an eye toward securing a viable place in the relationship-based global economy of the future.

It all begins with the machinery of networking. And that machinery must never stop.

1.3 How It All Started

I have 26 years of experience as a corporate HR management insider, outside agency recruiter, professional networker, adjunct professor/university lecturer on career management and career coach with an unusual but comon sense approach to networking and career management.

In addition, I have in-depth knowledge of international staffing, recruiting and networking which gives me the ability to both coach and consult with today's professionals and with executives around the world.

Obviously, I've seen the job search challenge from both sides of the interviewer's desk. I've been a corporate hiring manager and I've applied for positions with various companies. Along the way, I've seen many people struggle with the job search and interview process. As a result, I've discovered some of the more obscure pitfalls which trap people when they seek new jobs. (I'll be telling you more about those pitfalls in Chapter 9, *Putting It All Together and Troubleshooting.*)

This discovery convinced me to devote my life to helping as many people as possible avoid these traps. I also wanted individuals to experience a much higher success rate in landing the jobs they truly wanted. Because I knew I had a gift for teaching, training, and coaching, I decided to leave the corporate world and pursue my one true passion: the development of an organization committed to networking and helping people in transition. *And I didn't want to help these people merely get close to their next job —* **I wanted to help them nail it down!**

I started the ETP Network in 2004, at first just to eliminate the tedium of repeating nearly identical coaching and networking training to a long line of individuals. As the organization sprouted roots through e-mail exchanges, I made the decision to move to a Yahoo Groups-style forum to exchange documents, questions, and job search issues and then supplemented that with a weekly Sunday evening conference call. In the beginning, there were just a handful of call attendees. Today, our membership is in the thousands and growing steadily.

1.4   The View From 30,000 Feet

Here's a high level view of what the ETP Network is all about.

The ETP Network (Empowering Today's Professionals) is a **networking training organization** that teaches its members 1) how to network effectively and continuously improve their networking skills; 2) how to adopt a CEO-like mind-set for managing their careers; 3) how to create a powerful and compelling value proposition to make themselves as attractive as possible to decision-makers; and 4) how to fuse the three preceding skills into one megaskill while following a well-engineered and precisely targeted 7-Step Job Search Methodology. As part of this training, we teach members how to leverage the power of **advocates,** individuals who know you, trust you, and are willing to "connect the dots" for you if the circumstances warrant it. We leverage the power of these advocates to help you "network your way" into organizations or companies of interest. Let's start with our mission.

The ETP Network Mission

Our mission is to encourage, train, support, mentor and advise fellow CEOs in all areas of responsibility to their Personal Board of Directors. The key to a successful CEO enterprise is accomplishing these five goals:

1. Secure a job/business where passion and income intersect
2. Build a trusted personal network of 200+ people
3. Create a career backup plan
4. Generate multiple sources of income not in conflict **with the primary source**
5. Become a networking leader

Our Guiding Principle: *Own Your Career — Run It as a Business*

You take ownership of your career when you make the decision to run it as a business, complete with CEO (you), a Board of Directors (your family) plus R & D (networking and business intelligence), Sales & Marketing (interviews) and all other components that make up a fully functional organization. (I'll give you a more detailed breakout of your ME, Inc. business structure in Chapter 3, *The Mentality: Run Your Career as a Business.*)

At first, many individuals struggle with this paradigm. They think it's silly, uncomfortable, or inconvenient; some actually believe it's all three. But once they begin to apply it in real-life situations, they quickly see its value because it forces them to take responsibility for their actions. Suddenly, there is no room for excuses, no blaming others for bad decisions or errors in judgment. It finally hits them: Success or failure is totally in **their** hands.

Knowing that the safety and security of a Personal Board of Directors is your "corporate responsibility" every day is a powerful motivating force to keep you relentless in your job search and focused on your objectives.

Are you too tired to draft a **targeted resume?** Look at the faces of your children and think about how much they depend on you. Maybe you're too weary to track down one more well-matched opportunity? Listen to the voices of your loved ones and read their body language. **You owe it to them to be successful.**

Own Your Career. It's a powerful, emboldening statement. In three short words it captures the essence of the ETP Network's philosophy and serves as a powerful differentiator between the ETP Network and other more traditional networking groups. It also represents the difference between Black Hole thinking and CEO of ME, Inc. thinking.

It's easy to see why I chose it as the ETP Network's tagline!

1.5   Sizing Up the Competition

An excellent way to introduce anything new is to reveal comparisons between the "old way" and the "new way."

So as a first step in introducing you to the ETP Network, let's see how "we" compare with The Black Hole, a place where far too many of you have been spending far too much time in conducting your job searches:

The Black Hole	The ETP Network
Offers no ability to make connections with real, live people.	Based entirely on building a network work of trusted individuals.
Requires you to figure it out as you go; there is no instruction manual, guidance. There is no mechanism in place to provide feedback.	Provides step-by-step instruction and guidance
Success rate estimated to be 5 %	Success rate estimated to be 75 %
	Weekly instructional conference calls
	The ETP Network Toolbar, with "Smart Radar" alerts you to new job openings; alerts come directly to your computer desktop.
	High intolerance for excuses, whining, complaining, negativity; they waste precious time. Let's get serious about your search!
	Access to over 10 million professionals worldwide.

The advantages are obvious. Yet there are still far too many people slogging it out in The Black Hole. I believe the reason is simple: *they don't know there's a better way. They haven't heard about the ETP Network.*

They need to read this book and see how the ETP Network can help!

1.6 Features and Benefits —
What's in it for You?

New Member Orientation
When members first join the ETP Network, they receive orientation materials to guide them through the first steps. New members quickly find out if the ETP Network is a good fit for them. With its emphasis on personal accountability, a positive mental attitude, and a disciplined approach to career management, everyone starts out on equal footing and then either participates fully or drops out.

Connections to 10+ Million Professionals Globally
Over the past seventeen years, I have built up a network of thousands of contacts both here in North America and around the world. Right now, through the principle of "six degrees of separation", my network is estimated to be over 10 million professionals worldwide. *This is a network you will be able to access as you become actively engaged in our meetings, events, training programs, and member activities.*

Membership Conference Calls
The ETP Network currently holds weekly membership conference calls. The purpose of these calls is to provide training on the basics of networking, the CEO of ME, Inc. mind-set, the value proposition, and the **7-Step Job Search Methodology** itself. The topics are presented in rotation to ensure that new members are always given a chance to complete the training without excessive delay.

ETP Network Web Site: http://www.etpnetwork.com
We ask members to visit the ETP Network web site as frequently as possible for news, updates, and access to helpful articles and blogs. It's also the gateway for the

ETP Network "Member Lodge" (described on the next page).

ETPNEWS (Network Newsgroup)

We use an online forum to share news, information about upcoming events, articles, questions, and inspirational messages. Many members refer to this forum as a "safe haven" for the free flow of questions and ideas.

The 7-Step Job Search Methodology

This is the cornerstone of our entire program. If you become an ETP Network member, you will need to master this methodology as soon as possible. We lay it out clearly using illustrative scenarios, role-playing, and webinar reinforcement. We will soon be developing instructional videos to make the concepts and techniques a little easier to understand.

Coaching and Mentoring

I have been a career coach for over twelve years now. There are two ways in which you have access to me: 1) through our membership conference calls, there is always a "Q & A" session during which members can pose their questions and get direct answers; 2) retain my services privately ("for fee") if you want or need an extended one-on-one interaction.

Instructional Webinars

The ETP Network runs several high-quality instructional webinar programs. In the current rotation, we have: *The Seven Steps of the Job Search, the ETP Network Toolbar – Maximize Your Efficiency, Mastering the T-Letter (cover letter), Tips, Tools and Techniques for Your Use of LinkedIn and Tweet Your Way to Targeted Jobs or Business Opportunities.* More webinars are in development.

Job Aids and Instructional Materials

Members are encouraged to make use of the free job aids available for download on the ETP Network web site. Among them is a helpful job aid designed by Editor-in-Chief Chip Hartman which provides step-by-step, fully illustrated instructions for setting up a *value proposition* — with primary focus on a special type of cover letter called the "T-Letter." When you get to Chapter 4, *The Magnet: Your Value Proposition*, you'll see highlights from that job aid.

ETP Network Toolbar
(The ETP "Career Management Swiss Army Knife")

ETP Network Chief Operations Officer Carl Reid is obsessed with improving human effectiveness through technology. And nothing makes him happier than developing a product that helps members streamline their job search. Carl created the ETP Network Toolbar and it is now the most sought-after tool by members because of its ease of use, dashboard-style design plus the phenomenal "Smart Radar" system that pulls job descriptions directly onto a user's desktop **already customized for that user's core skill set.** *Wow !! Thanks, Carl!*

More About the ETP Network Toolbar

Every career professional or business owner needs constant business intelligence. The ETP Network toolbar acts as a personal assistant bringing you continuous, timely business updates. You can download your free copy of the ETP Network Toolbar from:

http://www.CareerManagementSwissArmyKnife.com

Powered by Conduit.com, running the ETP Network toolbar in Internet Explorer or Firefox web browsers provides the following powerful features:

- **Smart Radar (available for members only)**
  This tool continuously searches for job opportunities that match your skills while you're sleeping, watching TV reruns, or spending time with the family.

- **Salary and Cost of Living Calculators**
  If you're considering a relocation, this tool helps make informed business decisions.

- **Business Intelligence Tools**
  Quickly researching company background information and acquiring contact information for decision-makers is now a breeze.

- **Hot Buttons**
  Get "one click" access to sites like LinkedIn, Indeed.com, and the ETP Network news group.

- **ETP Network TV**
  Improve business, marketing and social media skills by watching videos right from the toolbar.

- **News Ticker**
  Keep up with ETP Network training and networking events. Clicking on a news item allows you to quickly register for an event or webinar.

- **And many more tools ...**
  Download the ETP Network Toolbar from:
  http://www.CareerManagementSwissArmyKnife.com

Networking Events

The ETP Network hosts many different networking events across the country. Aside from our own weekly meetings, we conduct seminars, webinars and speeches for other networking organizations plus job fairs, dinner meetings, charitable events and much more. All events are announced via the ETP Network web site.

ETP Network Locations
In the U.S.A. as of this book printing, the ETP Network has active chapters (usually multiple locations within a state) in Delaware, Florida, New Jersey, New York, Pennsylvania, North Carolina, Ohio, Washington, and Washington, DC. International locations include Canada, India, China, and the Philippines. Please see www.etpnetwork.com for the most current list.

Articles and Document Library
There are many good writers in the ETP Network. In fact that's how many members eventually become ETP Network Leaders. They share their research, views, insights, opinions, or perhaps their writing takes a more instructional tack. Either way, these members acquire good name recognition, especially if the membership regards their work as having consistently high value.

Video Library of Member-Produced Training Videos
We have videos of various events and instructional programs stored and archived on the ETP Network web site. These videos make great reference tools for new members and help to reinforce our core messages and principles.

Audio Library of Recorded Conference Calls
Currently, our audio library houses recordings in MP3 format for our weekly programs. If you cannot attend a particular call, it's easy enough to download the recording and listen to it the next day.

Guest Speakers
From time to time, we arrange for prominent guest speakers to join our conference calls. Most recently, we've had best-selling author and CEO of *JibberJobber.com*

Jason Alba speaks on the importance of managing relationships (handled by the online application he created called JibberJobber). He also delivered a blockbuster presentation based on his first book, _I'm On LinkedIn — Now What?_ (Copyright 2007, Happy About). In addition, author Don Gabor recently provided a first-rate presentation on "The Power of Small Talk", based on his best-selling book _Turn Small Talk into Big Deals_ (Copyright 2009, McGraw-Hill).

Newsletter, The Lamplighter
Our newsletter, _The Lamplighter_, keeps members wired in to late-breaking news about the organization, networking, the job search, social networking, and just about anything else relating to career management.

1.7 The Big Themes in ETP

We cover a lot of territory during our weekly programs and conference calls. In addition to the basic instruction and Q & A sessions, we spend a great deal of time discussing what I like to call "the big themes." These are topics that are deeply rooted in almost every phase of a successful job search and are therefore continuously analyzed and evaluated. Here is a list of the most important ones:

Making Effective Connections
Because we take networking very seriously, we take the _precursors_ of good networking very seriously too, including small talk, making connections and establishing trusted relationships. Small talk usually kicks off the connection process followed by a gradual mastery of the art of networking. I will show you the importance of

knowing when, how, and why to connect with others and how to build long-term, trusted relationships in Chapter 2, *The Machinery: Build, Track and Maintain Your Network.*

The Trust Matrix
As two individuals get acquainted and form a relationship based on genuine reciprocity, they establish a bond of trust. This trust deepens only as long as both parties continue to honor the relationship. Trust over time is a magic formula that can work wonders.

Relationships and Reciprocity
Good connections lead to good relationships. In business, relationships are everything. You'll know if a budding relationship has the chance to evolve into a deeper relationship if the *scales of reciprocity* remain balanced.

The Warm/Trusted Network
As you build a collection of trusted relationships, you are in reality building what the ETP Network calls a **warm, trusted network** (as opposed to The Black Hole where no one even knows you exist). It is this warm, trusted network that you will leverage when you need to find **advocates** for your job search.

Advocates are individuals who know you well and believe in you enough to put their reputations on the line by connecting you to key contacts within a company of interest. This is the real reason why The Black Hole fails and the ETP Network succeeds at helping people find jobs. We actually show members how to "network their way to their next job!" by leveraging the power of people, not machines.

Good vs. Bad Networking
There are many great books written on networking. One of the best is Keith Ferrazzi's <u>Never Eat Alone</u>

(Copyright 2005, Currency-Doubleday), the "final word" on networking in the view of ETP Network members and leaders. Keith explains with great clarity what constitutes good and bad networking and cites numerous examples of each (you'll probably find his chapter on the "Networking Jerk" enlightening, amusing, and maybe even disturbingly familiar).

Build Your Network Before You Need It
Most members quickly understand that having a warm trusted network beats anything you can find in The Black Hole. But they don't always recognize one key piece of network-management: ***You must have the network in place before you can tap it.***

This problem is especially noticeable just after landing a new job. Some people are tempted to abandon their network and their networking activities (including suspension of their ETP Network membership). They mistakenly believe they will remain with this new company for decades and have no further need for a network or networking. ***This is a huge mistake!***

> *It's a sure bet these folks missed the analysis of Thomas Friedman's book* <u>The World Is Flat</u> *located in the Introduction of this book. So please — if you're one of those people, go back and read the Introduction —* ***and do it now!***

Build Your Case for the Job
One of the greatest benefits of ETP Network membership is the extensive training we provide on how to build your case for a particular job.   With CEO of ME, Inc. thinking, the R & D Team of ME, Inc. handles the networking; the Sales & Marketing Team handles the interview and the ***value proposition.***
While that may sound easy, you still need the written

and verbal skills to defend the proposition that you are the most qualified person for the job. The written defense is made up of a **targeted resume** and a concise, compelling cover letter (such as the one known as a "T-Letter"). The oral defense will take place during the interview itself. I'll have more on this in Chapter 4, *The Magnet: Your Value Proposition*, and in Chapter 7, *The Interview and Negotiations*.

Your Value Proposition
In ETP Network terminology, your value proposition consists of three interrelated documents: 1) a suitable job description (one which confirms the matchup between your core skills and the position's stated requirements) 2) a targeted resume and 3) a cover letter (see Chapter 4).

Building Targeted Resumes and Cover Letters
Every day I see batches of resumes that come in for a particular job posting. And every day I become ill when I realize that the resumes I'm reviewing **don't even come close** to matching the core skills required for the position, at least not in the key timeframe of the most recent 3 – 5 years. I will teach you how to target your resumes and cover letters in such a way that they practically **scream** *"Relevance, Relevance, Relevance!"* (see Chapter 4).

You're Hired: Now What?
Fantastic! You've landed. The waiting is over — for now. The paychecks begin rolling in again. You turn your focus to doing the essential day-to-day work.

As crazy as this may sound, getting the job is actually a setback for some members. Why? Very simply, they fall into the *Complacency Trap*.

They begin to get comfortable in their new surroundings and feel there's no further need to attend networking events, conference calls, or webinars. I can understand the natural tendency to become complacent since many individuals are coming off very long periods of transition ... but I also know that it's a powerful trap just waiting to snag the unsuspecting newly employed person.

Here is the key to avoiding that trap: *Once you land, in my view, you're landing as the CEO of a business, the business of ME, Inc. Why would you suddenly slip back into the subservient role of a dependent employee again? Did you forget? Networking never stops. That needs to be your mantra. Learn more about this trap in Chapter 8, Once You've Landed.*

Leveraging the Power of Social Networks

Social networking sites like *LinkedIn*, *Twitter*, and *Facebook* are getting so much attention in the media these days that it's often difficult to keep track of them. Since they do play a role in your job search, I'll show you which ones will probably be most helpful and how to use them effectively. We'll examine the role of social networking in Chapter 10, *Social Networking: Be A Part of It.*

ETP Network is a Continuous Learning Laboratory

We are constantly using the ETP Network as a "learning laboratory" to test new applications, networking techniques, job search strategies, and lots more. On our conference calls, I like to engage attendees in "live" unscripted role-playing. Together, we shake out lots of misinformation and build up an extensive reserve of networking and job search knowledge.

Follow Up or Fail

This is where many job searchers simply get derailed. After a certain period of time following an important conversation, appointment, or interview, it's critical that you follow up with the "principals" of the meeting. *They have no obligation to keep your name in the forefront of their minds; it's your job to put it there* as a reminder that a decision is due so that both parties can move on.

Our Philosophy In A Nutshell

Imagine a warm summer day . You're at a beautiful fishing spot on a lake not far from where you live. There's a nice dock. The water looks delightful. You're anticipating a great afternoon of fishing.

Here is what we will do for you:

We'll bring the lounge chair, a pair of sunglasses, a sun hat, a portable radio, a cooler with refreshments in it, a fishing pole, some bait, and just about everything else you could imagine for a relaxing afternoon of fishing. If you need us to run to the store to get extra ice for the cooler, we'll even do that.

Here is what we will NOT do for you:
*We will **NOT** catch the fish for you. No, **YOU** will have to do the fishing. Maybe you'll be successful, maybe you won't. Either way, we're here to support you, guide you, offer suggestions and counseling; but we will **not** do the fishing for you.*

1.8 Adjustments to Attitude and Behavior

Mental Toughness
Actively taking on the role of a CEO running the business of your own career requires a certain level of mental toughness. Some of the decisions you'll need to make are difficult. Some of the people you'll encounter may be intimidating or stubborn. You'll have to deal with these situations effectively or risk losing control of your ME, Inc. business.

Think of mental toughness this way: It's the ability to do whatever is necessary to get the job done despite the obstacles that lie in your path. It requires an unusually high level of focus on the task at hand along with the ability to ignore distractions — all while maintaining an unwavering belief that you *can* accomplish what you *must* accomplish.

The Paradigm Shift to CEO of ME, Inc.
The paradigm that ETP members need to absorb is the shift from an employee mind-set (i.e., dependence on the boss, allegiance to a hierarchy of managers and the company itself) to a CEO of ME, Inc. mind-set (i.e., exercising complete control of their careers as successful, independent business owners). I will discuss this in detail in Chapter 3, *The Mentality: Run Your Career as a Business.*

Positive Mental Attitude
I believe that a positive mental attitude is one of the strongest weapons a person can have when facing adversity. It's taxing enough just trying to stay on top of all the work needed to carry out an effective job search. A positive mental attitude can change the way events

unfold so that they run more consistently in your favor. People who think negatively tend to induce negative events. People who think positively enjoy life more and, when faced with adversity, find the emotional where-withal to cope with it.

Our Program Is Binary: "Switch On" or "Switch Off"
Your ability to make a decision and stick to it is crucial to your success in this program. Those who spend every waking hour second-guessing themselves will be in for a very bumpy ride. You must begin to think of yourself as being in **switch on** or **switch off** mode — nothing in between. Make a decision. Stick to it. Try something new. If it fails, OK it fails, but then move on. If it works, decide what the next step is. Just avoid the choppy sea of indecision — it will sabotage your job search faster than anything else possibly could.

Do The Right Thing
ETP Network members need to make some tough choices. The Black Hole approach to the job search is an easy but ineffective escape; our approach is a monumental but rewarding challenge. I like to think that they make the decision to choose ETP is not just because it offers significantly better results but also because it's simply the right thing to do for their Personal Board of Directors and their own sense of self-esteem.

1.9   Online Tools and Resources

LinkedIn (www.LinkedIn.com)
LinkedIn is the database we use to manage our connections. If you are unfamiliar with LinkedIn, I recommend that you visit the site and get to know its features and functionality.

In this book, I will talk about "Level 1 connections" or "Level 2 connections" or "Level 3 connections." It will be important to have a working understanding of *LinkedIn* **before** you step through my job search methodology.

> *There are several excellent books that have been written about LinkedIn. One of the best ones was written by ETP Network member* **Jason Alba,** *also known for being the CEO of* **JibberJobber.com,** *an online relationship management tool that has helped millions with their job search and networking activities.*
>
> *Jason's book is:*
> <u>I'm On LinkedIn — Now What?</u>
> *(Copyright 2007, Happy About)*

Indeed (www.indeed.com)
We use Indeed.com as a starting point in the job search methodology to determine what positions are available in someone's geographic area that match pre-defined core skills. Indeed then searches its database of available jobs and returns a list of positions that should be considered strong possibilities for consideration.

Manta (www.manta.com)
Sometimes it's necessary to find information about a company to which you're applying. Manta's database provides company names, locations, phone numbers, and other helpful contact information.

Social Networking Web Sites
No one will dispute the sharp rise in popularity of sites like *LinkedIn, Twitter,* and *Facebook.* They are all relevant to the ETP Network job search methodology, however they don't all share the same priority.

ETP Network Leadership Team member Tom Kenny (who

has been instrumental in helping the organization learn more about *LinkedIn* and other social media) has an interesting way of framing this:

> "If you think of a continuum with LinkedIn at one end – representing the emphasis on business connections – and Facebook at the opposite end – representing the emphasis on social connections, then Twitter, as a "microblogging" site, would probably lie somewhere in the middle.
>
> LinkedIn is vital to the way we approach the job search; in fact the 7-Step Job Search Methodology absolutely requires it. Twitter and Facebook are not as critical to the search methodology per se, but they can be valuable connection venues for those who master their functions.
>
> A word of caution: For those considering the use of Twitter and Facebook to establish connections and relationships, be aware that there is a growing trend among hiring managers to search these sites for candidates who have made an application at their companies. Since Twitter and Facebook posts are visible for public consumption (unless overridden with privacy settings), you must avoid posting sensitive information or information that might be easily misinterpreted and viewed as unfavorable."

I will discuss Social Networking in more detail in Chapter 10, *Social Networking: Be a Part of It!*

1.10   Summary and Scoreboard

You've just read Chapter 1. In winning the race for 21st century jobs, you now know the following:

- The ETP Network helps professionals in transition

manage their careers as a business.

- The ETP Network offers a broad base of support for those who take on the responsibility for managing their careers as a business.
- There are four "core components" that drive the ETP Network Job Search System:

  1.**The Machinery:** Build, Track and Maintain Your Network
  2.**The Mentality:** Run Your Career as a Business
  3.**The Magnet:** Your Value Proposition
  4.**The Methodology:** Follow the 7-Step Job Search Methodology

CORE CHAPTERS											
1	2	3	4	5	6	7	8	9	10	11	12

You now have three options:

1. Ignore the rest of the book and move on to other things.
2. Slide back into the dead-end comfort of The Black Hole.
3. Move on to Chapter 2 to learn about connecting, networking, and developing the relationships that will help you network your way into your next job or attract your next client.

It's Your Decision.

Chapter 2

The Machinery: Build, Track and Maintain Your Network

2.1 Networking: The Machinery That Drives Business

My wife took her wrist watch to the local jeweler for repair. The store was very busy, but eventually she found her way to the glass display case with a smiling salesman behind it.

"How can I help you?"
he asked.

Stop.

What an utterly brilliant question! "How can I help you?" "What can I do for you?" "Is there some way I can be of service to you?" "What is it that I can do to help you achieve your objectives?"

Theoretically, you could read that last paragraph, study it, let it penetrate into the deepest crevices of your mind, then move on to Chapter 3 *because you've just captured the essence of good, solid business networking!*

That's right — **the secret to great networking lies in what you can do to help others!**

But now that you know this, don't skip ahead; in fact, don't skip anything. Why? You'd be surprised how many people still cling to the belief that networking is all about "connecting with others so they can help me find a job." *Unfortunately that's not networking, that's spamming a fellow human being.* People who do this should put themselves in the role of the spamee and consider how it might feel if the roles were reversed. Let's just think of it as the **Golden Rule of Networking** and to be an effective networker, it's a rule you must follow.

What it comes down to is this: You must discover what you can do, offer, or share that ingratiates you with others and makes them genuinely look forward to your next meeting. Doing this consistently brands you as someone of interest, someone who is truly worth knowing. As you consistently treat people in this manner, it's no accident that they look for opportunities to reciprocate.

And it all starts with the "small talk," the key to making those first connections!

2.2 Small Talk: Getting to Know You ... Maybe

It's surprising to discover how many people consider "small talk" irrelevant to networking. I couldn't disagree more. When I think back on all my first-time encounters, not one of them would have been initiated without the use of small talk. The bottom line is there's nothing small about it. I won't spend a lot of time discussing the subject here; instead I'll refer you to some books that handle the subject brilliantly. They were written by my good friend and ETP Network member **Don Gabor:**

- <u>Turn Small Talk Into Big Deals</u>
  (Copyright © 2009 by McGraw-Hill)
- <u>How To Start A Conversation And Make Friends</u>
  (Copyright © 2001 by Fireside)
- <u>Talking With Confidence for the Painfully Shy</u>
  (Copyright © 1997 by Three Rivers Press)

Don understands the value of small talk and he is a master at it. Although that may not sound like a spectacular achievement on its own, the art of small talk determines how well you will form connections — and the relationships that result from them!

2.3 Connections: When It's You and Someone Else

I have a special reverence for those occasions when I meet a person and step into his or her life for the very first time. You never know what surprises await. The person you're about to meet may have won a Pulitzer Prize, climbed Mt. Everest, or served time for bank robbery. As a person's story gradually unfolds before you, it will be quite easy to tell if there are sparks of mutual interest that could ignite for future encounters.

Whenever you first meet someone, you take a risk — but that's how all good relationships start. They start with an element of chance, the chance that the other person might become a good friend or perhaps a trusted business associate based on common interests, shared experiences, and perhaps some good old-fashioned intuition.

But if you're not willing to risk a first encounter, there's little hope of developing any relationships. Call me foolish, but I relish these opportunities because, even when the worst-case scenario **does** occur, I still end up learning a great deal about human nature. There is never any real failure in the *connection laboratory*, just occasional setbacks.

In reality, first-time connections are golden opportunities for future relationships and in the business world, connections and relationships are everything. Just try conducting business without them! You won't get very far — and that will be especially true in the 21st century jobscape where the opportunities for business growth will be heavily dependent on the strength and abundance of personal relationships.

Determine Someone's Wants / Needs / Desires (W/N/D)
Let me share a special technique that creates an immediate bond with another person. The technique is to get people talking about their W/N/D (wants/needs/desires). It's an incredible weapon in your networking arsenal.

This is how it plays out in conversation: You pick up a casual remark about selling Girl Scout cookies or coaching the swim team, for example. **That** then gives you a hook on which to hang questions, express interest, and fuel a conversation. The best part is that your desire to learn about someone else frequently triggers reciprocal inquiries because people are naturally curious. Presto! You've just established a connection. Whether it deepens or dissolves from this point on is totally up to the two of you.

Uncover a Person's Passion and Build an
Instantaneous Bond
Keith Ferrazzi, author of <u>Never Eat Alone,</u> believes that if you uncover a person's true passion, you have a golden

opportunity to bond with that individual since you'll be connecting on a powerful, emotional level. Indeed, most people will freely share information about their passions and interests.

FORM = Family / Occupation / Recreation / Money
(FORM = GOALS)
Another useful formula for making connections is the FORM Equation. Get someone talking about any of the four topics above and you'll be connecting in record time. Why? People love to talk about the powerful motivations that propel them toward their life goals.

Nurture the Budding Relationship
Once you establish an interesting connection with someone, nurture it with periodic follow-up. Connections can be solid but fleeting; if you sense there is substance to a new connection, don't miss the chance to reinforce it by making a phone call or two. Nurturing a good connection is the best way to solidify it into a trusted, long-term relationship.

> *Throughout this book, a common theme will be:* **Follow up.** *Don't allow yourself to forget this critical step. In my view, the failure to follow up with newly made acquaintances — and even people with whom you already share a trusted relationship — accounts for almost half of all relationship failures.*

Play It Low-Key With Bad Connections
Many of us carry a certain amount of negative baggage. But if it consistently oozes into the conversation with someone you've just met, consider an early exit. People who radiate negativity drag everyone else down with them. Who needs **that** when you're already hip-deep in a job search?

The bottom line is this: If you decide that a new connection isn't going to work, politely head for the door. Confrontations rarely produce positive results.

2.4 Connections: When You are the Connector

Your Reputation Is On the Line

Sooner or later, you will find yourself in the role of connector, that is, you will be asked by someone to "connect him or her" with someone you know. When this happens, carefully weigh the value of the connection. Make sure you understand the worth each individual brings to the table. Finally, evaluate whether the connection truly serves the best interests of *all* parties, *including you!*

Protect the Connector

I am ultra-careful about this principle and I believe you should be, too.

Whenever I "go out on a limb" to connect Person "A" with Person "B", I am exposing myself to *three different levels of risk:*

Level 1: The risk that she may not follow through on making the contact as we agreed

Level 2: The risk that the *value proposition* she offers for the connection may not be adequate

Level 3: The risk that she might behave in an inappropriate manner that could jeopardize the relationship I have with the individual of interest

Most of us have been in this kind of situation before. Here's a little story that illustrates the risks assumed by connectors:

> *It's a quiet, peaceful Friday evening. I'm looking forward to a relaxing weekend with my family. Suddenly the phone starts ringing off the hook in the den. I can tell by the area code on the caller ID that my weekend may be off to a rocky start. It's Ted from Cincinnati.*

Rod:
"Rod Colón ..."

Ted:
"Rod? It's Ted from Cincinnati. How are you?"

Rod: *{long pause}... "Reasonably well, Ted, thanks for asking. What can I do for you?"*

Ted:
"Rod, I know we've been out of touch for a long time now, but my situation is very, very serious. I really need you to connect me with Jack Talbott over at MangoTango Electronics. I don't have time to attend ETP meetings or events because I belong to a new bowling league and we can only get the alleys on weekday evenings. Please just make the connection for me and I'll take it from there. I know this is a good fit for me."

Rod:
"Ted, listen: I shared my position on this once before, remember? You really need to understand it from my point of view. It's true, I've seen your resume but I don't really know you all that well. It took me 8 years to build my network, a network which I now freely share with everyone who joins the ETP Network. It consists of thousands upon

thousands of people who I know very well. They are valued contacts."

Ted:

"Yeah, I know, but I won't let you down, I promise."

Rod:

"OK, let me go at it from a different angle — what you're saying is that you want me to connect you, someone I hardly know, with a trusted member of my network. Why would I want to do that? No offense, but what if you turn out to be a jerk or something? Then what happens to me the next time I speak with Jack Talbott? Do you think he's going to be glad to speak with me? I doubt it. In fact he may decide that our relationship has taken a hit because I've referred a jerk to him."

Ted:

"Rod, I guarantee you, I'm not a jerk. I absolutely guarantee it. Just make the connection, OK?"

Rod:

"Ted, it took a long time for me to build this network. But there must be guidelines for using it, since I — as the connector — have the most to lose in making this type of connection. Of the three parties involved in this potential connection — you, Jack, and me — I'm the one with the greatest risk. You **DO** understand that, don't you?"

Ted:

"Of course I understand, Rod. But I was thinking that just this once, maybe you could bend the rules a little and give Jack a call and tell him about me. I know he'll be interested."

Rod:
(Click)

Suggested Connection Protocols

When you're ready to be the connector, consider the following connection protocols. If you can, it's always best to do the connecting in person. But other protocols can be just as effective:

- Fellowship — arrange a lunch if possible (strongest)
- Conference call — set up a conference call and introduce the two parties
- Send an e-mail message to the party being introduced and copy the person looking to be introduced with details and the reason for the connection
- Give one or both sides contact information for the other without being involved (weakest)

Connecting Individuals with Businesses
(the B2B Model)

The other scenario (with you as the connector) is when you connect individuals with businesses. Here, in what might be considered a "business-to-business model", the role of a connector or networker now becomes what's known as the *channel partner.* The underlying techniques remain the same, but in this case, the connector typically derives financial gain through a pre-agreed arrangement between the parties.

2.5   Connections Lead to Relationships

The Trust Factor

The next time you find yourself in a bookstore, head over to the *Networking and Business* section and look for a book called The Speed of Trust by Stephen M. R. Covey (Copyright 2006, CoveyLink,LLC). Many networking professionals consider it the definitive work on trust in relationships, particularly how trust is earned and how it's lost.

Reciprocity Keeps Relationships Balanced
All solid relationships are built on trust and reciprocity. But in the beginning, many people need to ask themselves a key question to find out if a relationship will be worth nurturing. That is:

What's In It For Me? (WIIFM)

If there is perceived value in the relationship, most people will have no difficulty in building the bonds of trust and the bridges of reciprocity to keep the relationship growing and evolving over time.But please note that I said "*most* people" ... there are some individuals who don't grasp the need for reciprocity and their selfish behavior quickly dissipates any initial interest others may have in them.

This "breed" of individuals is what author Keith Ferrazzi (Never Eat Alone) identifies as **networking jerks.** These lost souls have no clue as to what reciprocity really means. They travel through life with their self-centered entitlement mentality on full display, completely unaware that they openly and publicly alienate others and prevent connections from developing into relationships (or preventing connections from occurring in the first place).

After identifying them as such, the safest method for dealing with networking jerks is to simply ignore them. There is no need for a confrontation with someone whose personality doesn't gel with yours.

Trust Maintenance

Now let's take a look at some specific actions you can take to maintain trust and keep a relationship alive:

- Be direct, open and honest in all communications with others
- Maintain a level of respect for others that they begin to view as your "brand"
- Admit mistakes when you make them
- Demonstrate appreciation and gratitude for the efforts of others
- Protect the privacy of others; always keep private information confidential
- Establish a track record for getting results
- Set realistic benchmarks for improving your own performance and value
- Demonstrate a willingness to confront difficult problems "head on"
- Set up mutually agreed "accountability milestones"; i.e., a healthy relationship allows each member to voice expectations without hurt or hesitation
- Demonstrate your prowess as a troubleshooter but allow for divergent points of view
- Keep promises and commitments and establish a solid track record of unquestionable reliability
- Be willing to risk the extension of trust to others

2.6   Relationships Build Networks

In the ETP Network, the term 'networking' has a special meaning. It's the machinery that drives everything we do and it's the cornerstone of our unique job search methodology. The ability to forge connections with new people in an appropriate way is critical to your success as a business owner committed to the enterprise known as managing your own career.

The list below summarizes my thoughts on networking. It comes directly from Never Eat Alone by Keith Ferrazzi. I use it frequently when I speak to large groups because for many people these points are often brand new:

- **Don't keep score**
  We know and understand reciprocity and we recognize its critical importance for healthy, successful relationships. But the scales of reciprocity don't necessarily require an absolute balance; sometimes we give more, sometimes we take more. If it all ends up in overall balance, there's no need to keep score.

- **What's your mission?**
  To be a good networker, you must not only know your own personal mission, but have the ability to communicate it in a way that stimulates interest and the desire for follow up.

- **Build your network before you need it**
  You recognize the need to build a good, reliable network. The point here is simply to make sure that you build it, sustain it, and maintain it long before it becomes necessary for you to leverage it due to some business or professional need. The metaphor here is "dig the well before you need the water." Enough said.

- **Become a fearless networker**
  Who are the most successful networkers?
  Most experts agree that the best networkers are
  those who can step outside of their own safety
  zones and project a bold, even occasionally
  audacious persona in their social interactions.
  If nothing else, they clearly get remembered.

- **Do your homework**
  As you continue to expand your network, you'll
  want to learn as much as you can about "people of
  interest" you'd like to include. Knowing something
  about their interests, hobbies, and "downtime
  activities" makes it much easier to engage them
  in small talk.

- **Develop a list**
  One of the best features of building lists is that it
  reveals just how extensive your network really is.
  Many people forget that networks are built across
  all different zones of daily life, e.g., work, family,
  hobbies, etc... You probably know more people
  than you realize!

- **The warm call in 15 seconds**
  When connecting with people by phone, always
  mention who the connector was (this establishes
  trust and credibility) and the reason for the
  connection. As with most other aspects of
  networking, be sure to follow up.

- **Managing the gatekeeper**
  In most business environments, gatekeepers are
  individuals such as secretaries, administrative
  assistants, etc... who provide access to key people.
  Knowing how to interact with gatekeepers will

help you to maximize access to those you're trying to reach.

- **Your network is like a muscle**
  You've heard it all your life: To make muscles grow, make sure they get adequate exercise. There is absolutely no difference in terms of net works; the more you manage your network (e.g., "pinging", updating contact information, sending greetings for special occasions, etc...) the stronger and tighter it becomes. If you truly want a stronger, healthier network, make sure you "work it" every day.

- **Share your passions**
  While it used to be perceived as a weakness, those who display a genuine passion for their interests are actually very highly regarded. If you are some one who enjoys exuding energy and enthusiasm for what interests you, the rule of thumb for 21st century professionals is "go for it." Just make sure it's genuine; this one cannot be faked.

- **Follow up or fail**
  The failure to follow up on e-mails, meetings, phone calls, etc... is the biggest single source of failure for most job seekers. They forget all too easily that it is their responsibility to keep their names and faces *fresh* in the minds of would-be employers or decision-makers. When thinking about this, place emphasis on the word "fresh."

- **Attend conferences but do your research first**
  Conferences and major events are great opportunities for networking but they have proportionally less value if they are sponsored by organizations

with little relevance to your own business interests. Check out the sponsors, make a few inquiries,
and chances are you'll then be connecting with
people who have clearly similar interests to yours.

- **Connecting with connectors**
  There are connectors and then there are "super-
  connectors." Super-connectors are those individuals who have mastered the connection process to a
  level at which it's done almost reflexively and
  spontaneously. Being able to connect with a "super-
  connector" has obvious advantages and building a
  solid relationship with a "super-connector" has some
  highly distinctive long-term advantages.

- **Expanding your circle through partnering**
  Build your network carefully. Making connections
  involves a certain level of risk. Not every connection
  will become a relationship. It's helpful to regard
  newly developed connections as "potential partners"
  — just be sure you know when to cut the ties if you
  determine the relationship cannot be realistically
  sustained.

- **Stay in touch – all the time**
  One of the most critical things to do in building
  a network is to simply stay in touch with every
  member. You need to be willing to "ping" your
  network periodically (see below).

2.7 Network Tracking and Maintenance

By now, you should be intent on developing a strong, expansive network of trusted individuals who will support you in your efforts to manage your career as a business. And you must be prepared to offer others your support in return.

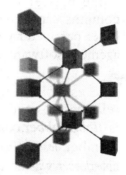

For some people, the relationship represents an objective achieved, a goal met, or an endpoint reached. This is good because they've taken the process from connection to relationship to trusted relationship, to a warm trusted network.

Master Networkers
But there is another group of people for whom networking goes beyond a task that's completed in order to execute a job search: They insist on being able to manage their relationships and monitor the frequency with which contact is maintained. These are the people who truly cultivate and value each individual relationship. This is an elite group of individuals known as *master networkers,* and anyone can join this group; you just have to want it bad enough. Master networkers are well-schooled in the *Seed / Feed / Weed* cycle of relationship maintenance. *Seeding* is the early stage connection that shows great promise. *Feeding* is the day-to-day maintenance of each relationship. *Weeding* represents those times — much as we may not like to think of them — that we need to prune back our network because some

of its branches are not all that productive. Good networkers recognize the value of pruning since it provides additional nourishment to the productive branches.

Some master networkers set up spreadsheets with columns capturing the who/what/when/date, and every other parameter you can think of. Some use contact management software available on various web sites.

One especially interesting online tool for managing relationships and capturing an impressive level of detail is *JibberJobber.com* designed by author and ETP Network member *Jason Alba* (mentioned throughout this book). *JibberJobber* was designed specifically for those who believe that nurturing relationships is an active, ongoing task that gets woven into their daily routine as a habit. If you're a serious networker, you will want to "test drive" this tool and make use of the outstanding training resources that Jason has provided on the *JibberJobber* web site, **www.jibberjobber.com**

The Ping Principle
Keith Ferrazzi uses this term in <u>Never Eat Alone</u>. It states that once you've got your network set up, you can't just forget it, fall completely out of touch, and assume that the relationship with person "X" will retain its original value. You must make *periodic contact* to keep the relationship alive.

Individuals who fall off the radar due to your negligence in pinging them may not be eager to rejoin your active community, so don't take the risk.

Be aware that failure to receive an occasional *ping* from you **might** be interpreted as a loss of interest in the relationship and that can have considerable downhill consequences. To prevent this, take an action step.

For some of our members, pinging is as simple as recording a contact's birthday in their *JibberJobber* database and then setting up regular time intervals to send an e-mail, make a phone call, or invite someone to lunch.

2.8 You Have a Warm, Trusted Network: Now What?

ETP Network members always develop above-average networking skills; that's one of several personal missions I have. But most of them also begin to realize that effective networking offers something else, too.

It offers an opportunity to gather business intelligence, cultivate relationships in selective areas of a particular industry, and gather valuable contact information.

What's the value of all this? At some point, this network-generated information might just produce business for you. Why on earth would you NOT want to do it?

The real value of all this intelligence-gathering will become clear when you begin to probe the contents of Chapter 6, *The Hidden Job Market*.

2.9   Repeat After Me ...

OK, so you know the basics of connections, relationships, networks, and networking. You need to be sure to observe the following guidelines in all of your networking endeavors:

- Never think about making connections because of what you believe others can do for you; approach it in terms of what you can do to support the goals of others.

- Never try to use networking as a means of asking for employment. Instead, use networking to ask for advice, guidance, or suggestions for what some "next steps" might be given your particular situation.

- If you are placed in the role of a connector (i.e., you will, at someone's request, be asked to connect person "A" with person "B"), make sure you understand the requestor's *value proposition*, i.e., what it is that they bring to the table for the benefit of the relationship. If you believe their value proposition is weak or inadequate, politely decline the request to make the connection on the grounds that you, as the connector, have the most to lose if the relationship doesn't work out well.

  Note: I'm using the term 'value proposition' here in the generic business sense, not the ETP Network-specific sense as you'll learn about in Chapter 4. While the two are close, they're not identical.

- Get comfortable with small talk; you'll need it to grease the wheels of first-time connections.

- Carefully manage the trusted networks you build. Treat each relationship as if it's the most important link in your chain. Ping your network regularly.

- Follow up or fail. Soon you'll be thinking of your career as a business owner (the CEO of ME, Inc.), and so this is now a "corporate responsibility", not an idle task on a "to do" list.

- Build your network before you need it. Never become complacent; when you find yourself in transition, have the network already in place to help support you and guide you to your next position.

- Networking (as part of the business of managing your career) NEVER STOPS.

2.10   An Important Conclusion

So why did we just spend an entire chapter discussing networking, connections, and relationships? I'll be specific:

*Once we get into the 7-Step Job Search Methodology (Chapter 5), you will need to find **advocates,** i.e., people who can help you "network your way" into a particular organization or company. Without the use of advocates, you might as well spend your time in The Black Hole.*

If your networking or connecting skills are rusty, you may have to spend some additional time in developing them so that you can establish appropriate advocate relationships with confidence when they're needed.

*Since you can't possibly know **now** just who those future advocates will be, you'll have to treat **everyone** you meet as though they are a potential advocate.*

*Without the use of advocates, your job search methodology will either fail you or at the very least slow you down...**way down.***

2.11 Summary and Scoreboard

You've just read Chapter 2. In winning the race for 21st century jobs, you now know the following:

- There are special "mechanics" of how to make connections and form trusted relationships

- Trust and reciprocity are key for any meaningful relationship

- There are various scenarios in which connections are made; and don't forget about "protecting the connector."

- The value of tracking and maintaining your network.

	CORE CHAPTERS										
1	2	3	4	5	6	7	8	9	10	11	12
▲	▲										

You now have three options:

1. Ignore the rest of the book and move on to other things.
2. Slide back into the dead-end comfort of The Black Hole.
3. Move on to Chapter 3 to learn about the business paradigm we'll use to direct and coordinate your job search.

It's Your Decision.

Chapter 3
The Mentality:
Run Your Career as a Business

3.1 All About Paradigms

Ona camping trip in the Rocky Mountains "many years ago", ETP Network Editor-in-Chief Chip Hartman had the misfortune of stepping into a pool of quicksand along the banks of a slow-moving river. I'll let Chip tell the story:

*"We broke camp around 7 am and headed toward the river. The embankment was so steep we had to run down the path to reach the water's edge. We **thought** we were running out onto a wide sandy area along the river bank, but it wasn't. With the very first step, three of us sank into the muck at least six inches. Every time we tried to remove one leg, the other would sink deeper. In less than a minute, we were almost waist-deep. Then we remembered the advice of a forest ranger only a few days earlier: 'If you step into quicksand, you can escape by either lying backward or forward on it. It's denser than water so you can actually float **higher** in it than water as long as you're calm and don't make any sudden thrashing movements. You*

*can **float** your way out of it.' **But how could we do***
***something so preposterous and illogical?** There was*
no time for debate. We either had to float our way out or
risk a horrible death. One by one we tried, very gently.
Little by little we paddled out with our arms and reached an
area were there was secure footing underneath."

Pretty frightening, isn't it? But Chip's quicksand story provides an interesting insight into paradigms. Many of us were brought up to believe the Hollywood stereotype of quicksand victims thrashing upright in the muck, yelling and screaming as they sank deeper and deeper, gasping for that final breath before slipping under the surface. It was a grim, terrifying way to die — ***and we all bought it!***

Which proves how easy it is to cling to long-held beliefs, especially if they go unchallenged for a long time. And that makes me wonder: How many **other** beliefs do we hold as absolutes, absolutes that could be easily debunked if a better explanation came along? In Chip's case, the need to quickly change long-held beliefs may have saved his life. What could it do for you?

In this chapter, I'm going to ask you to let go of the belief that so many job seekers cling to — searching for jobs in The Black Hole — and adopt an entirely new way of thinking about career management.

Let's get to work.

3.2   The CEO of ME, Inc. Paradigm

The CEO of any company runs the company. CEOs direct all critical operations such as sales and marketing, research and development, strategy, finance, corporate culture, human resources, community affairs, public relations, and so on.

CEOs are primarily responsible for setting the corporate strategy and vision. They decide which products to introduce into which markets and against which competitors. CEOs decide how the company will brand itself and differentiate itself in the marketplace.

Ultimately, the CEO is responsible for the success or failure of the company.

Here are some key CEO responsibilities that you must learn to incorporate into your job search:

<u>As the CEO of your career you will:</u>

• Learn to partition your responsibilities to ensure that all critical operations are carried out and none get overlooked. For example, your Research & Development Department will be in charge of net working — making connections, digging up new leads, gathering business information, etc... Right from the start, anything you do that's part of this effort is processed in the R & D "department" of your mind. Likewise, your Sales & Marketing Department will oversee the development of a powerful value proposition and various parts of the 7-Step Job Search Methodology until every task is properly niched.

• Take responsibility for making tough decisions — there's just no way around this. Tough decision-making is a skill with tremendous short- and long-term benefits. It trains your mind to weigh options before you commit to a course of action.

- Accept the consequences of your tough decisions — both good and bad. You can savor the good results and analyze why the bad results occurred. Most importantly, don't waste time beating your self up when a decision yields poor results. Pick up the pieces and move on. Learn from every aspect of the failure experience because it will move you closer to winning the race for 21st century jobs.

- Bring a new level of personal accountability to your job search. Why? Because you have a "governing body" to which you now have ultimate responsibility: your Personal Board of Directors (e.g., spouse, family, extended family, significant other, etc...).

Still not convinced your job search can benefit from thinking like a CEO? Are you saying, "Why bother? This sounds like a whole lot of work for very little benefit."

If that's how you see it, consider this: For every terrific opportunity you identify — and for which you're qualified — there could be hundreds, maybe thousands of others competing for the same position. But there's one critical difference: *Most of **them** fail to adopt the "I'm in charge" attitude and **their** race for the finish line becomes a mediocre performance at best.* They remain mired in the "employee mind-set", a part of the Black Hole crowd that inevitably lags behind in the race to get the job that **you are busy targeting.** And while most of us don't **want** others to fail, *there's nothing wrong with capitalizing on the inept business decisions of others to gain a tactical advantage whenever possible.* In other words, if **you** are thinking like a business owner and your competitors aren't, you have a significant edge over them in the race for 21st century jobs. ***Do not fail to leverage it!***

Will you absorb this paradigm shift overnight? No. In a week? Unlikely. In a month? Maybe. People internalize it at very different rates. Most of our members can tell rather quickly if they are cut out to be the CEO of ME, Inc.

The good news is that this mental model *will* work if you *make* it work.

3.3 The Back Story on the CEO of ME, Inc. and the ETP Network

---

When I was a Human Resources recruiter at J. P. Morgan, I became fascinated with the success rate achieved by recruiting agencies. They always had a sharp eye for talent and a good understanding of what the client wanted. This didn't really surprise me — after all, it's what made them good business owners. In addition, they asked great questions, and when they submitted a proposal (i.e., a resume) for a client, it was **dead on.** But what I really wanted to know was what made them so outstanding at their work.

I used to visit these agencies and talk with people at their desks in an attempt to learn from them. They gave me an almost exclusive look at what went on behind the scenes. I quickly saw that the agency had clear-cut business divisions, e.g., R & D, Sales & Marketing, etc... and they were executing daily operations just like a well-managed company.

I began to ask myself: If this successful business model worked so well for recruiting agencies, what would happen if we adapted it for *individuals?* Could it work? This is how I came up with the idea of combining good, solid networking skills, a CEO of ME, Inc. mind-set, the development of a powerful value proposition and integrating all three of them into a logically-sequenced job search methodology. *This power combination was the first step in giving my methodology the "teeth" it needed to put The Black Hole out of business.*

By requiring ETP Network members to be accountable to their Personal Board of Directors, they must confront and resolve whatever conflict might exist between "low road negative thinking" and the "high road well-being of their own families." When you realize that you're making smart, solid and informed decisions that are in the best interests of your family, a whole spectrum of possibilities opens up. **You're doing the right thing — and you know it!**

3.4 Commit to It Then Hold Yourself Accountable

The key to developing ME, Inc. is the idea of reframing the self-image of the employee (or job seeker) from the powerless "employee" to the powerful, in-charge CEO of ME, Inc.

The following passage is a *commitment pledge* I drafted to help me internalize the shift in thinking from employee to business owner for my own Personal Board of Directors. Maybe it will give you some ideas for developing your own commitment pledge and holding yourself accountable for seeing it through:

As CEO of Rod, Inc., I have responsibilities to run my business for the benefit of my Board of Directors (Maria, Rod III, Nick, Alicia and extended family). I have business decisions to make geared at maximizing my profitability in selling my **value proposition.**

I have no excuses, just a business to run. Jobs, employers, layoffs, etc. are not personal, just part of business. I do not think of "giving an honest day's work for a day's pay" (although I do that and more). Instead, I am a business owner providing an honest service at a good price to a valued client.

In order to get a client, I need to establish my value proposition, evaluate the geographic market for what I am selling (my skills and experience), and understand that I may need to modify one or the other depending on supply and demand. In general, as a business, I need:

1) Something productive to do on Monday morning that I'm looking forward to on Sunday night

2) A back-up plan

3) Multiple sources of income that do not conflict with my primary source of income

4) A network of at least 200 people that I care about and who care about me

3.5 Dealing With the 9 − 10 Inches Between Your Ears

To be successful with the CEO of ME, Inc. paradigm, it's important to get comfortable with the "9 − 10 inches between your ears" where all thought is processed. You have a surprising amount of  control over what happens in there. Let me review some concepts that will be helpful as you begin to acquire the CEO mind-set.

Mental Toughness

Taking on the role of a CEO running a business requires a certain level of mental toughness. What is mental toughness? It's the ability to do whatever is necessary to get the job done despite the obstacles that may lie in your path. It requires an unusually high level of focus on the task at hand along with the ability to ignore real or potential distractions. Many people equate mental toughness with the ability to cope with life's most challenging problems.

We'll take a closer look at mental toughness and a positive mental attitude in Chapter 11, *The Awesome Power of Attitude and Behavior.*

This Program Is Binary In Nature: Switch On/Switch Off

Your ability to make a decision and stick to it is crucial to making this program work. Those who spend most of their waking hours second-guessing themselves will be in for a very bumpy ride.

Your mind must absorb the CEO of ME, Inc. paradigm in either **switch on** or **switch off** mode — nothing in between. Make a decision. Stick to it. Try something new. If it fails, move on. If it works, decide what the next step should be. Don't allow yourself to get caught up with endless indecision — it will sabotage your job search faster than anything else possibly could.

Accept Responsibility

Learning the 7-Step Job Search Methodology in Chapter 5 will be time-consuming but not difficult. But putting it into practice without making at least **some** mistakes the first time out will be quite challenging. Fight the temptation to blame anyone but yourself. **You're a business owner. You** made the error, so accept it, learn from it, then simply move on.

Do The Right Thing

In the ETP Network, this expression has special meaning. For members, it is the guideline that keeps people committed to the task of following the CEO of ME, Inc. program — even when instinct and emotion pull them in the opposite direction. For leaders, it's the axiom that keeps them focused on making the ongoing contributions to keep the organization running smoothly.

3.6   Side-By-Side Mind-Set Comparison

It's time to make some visual comparisons between the old-style "employee" mind-set and the new "CEO of ME, Inc." mind-set. The following chart gives you a good idea of how the two approaches stack up:

Old Employee Approach	New CEO of ME, Inc. Approach
Job Search	Market your skills to create and stay open to multiple opportunities. Keep many options available.
Network only when *you* need a job. *Then* wonder why it takes so long to land a position.	Constantly market and network inside and outside your organization. Reach out to your network and find 1 opportunity per day.
Prepare your resume	Prepare proposal to present skills/ benefits that pass the "6 second" acid test. Always carry your business cards.
Initial interview.	Business meeting with a potential client.
Interviewer asks questions to find out why they should hire you.	Ask questions to identify the client's business requirements. Client answers determine whether or not you whould work for them.
You are placed in the beggar's seat and asked what salary you are looking for.	Never give away your bottom line. "I would consider any reasonable offer betweem [give your range], not a specific amount." (Places *you* in the driver's seat.)
Interviewer wraps up interview	You go for the gusto with a killer close to make a memorable impression on the client. Close with your 3 best skills that match the client's needs. " I would like to give you 3 reasons why I am the best resource for this position, out of any person you have interviewed or will interview."
Salary & Benefits Offer	Contract Negotiation. Ask for everything. Then compromise at the negotiation table. Always wait until the next day to accept offers.

Similarly, a CEO thinks and speaks like a CEO. The old business jargon no longer represents a viable means of communication for 21st century business. The following chart compares the old-style terminology and thought pattern with the modern CEO-style:

Terminology/Thinking	New Terminology/Thinking
Employer	One of several clients
Employee	CEO of ME, Inc.
Interview Process	Selling
Job Offer	Negotiable Offer
Job Search	Open to Opportunities
Landing a Job	Closing a Deal
Business / team / person alignment	Networking
Employee evaluation	Development Plan
Email, Telephone, Dress Code, Speaking	Marketing Tools
Responding to a job advertisement	Providing a Value Proposition
Cover Letter	Executive Summary
Resume	Proposal
Organizational Chart	Business Intelligence about Key Players
Pitching an Idea	Making a Presentation
Networking	Cultivating mutually beneficial relationships
Being a Team Player	Collaborating
Email Signature	Electronic Business Card

Keeping People in the Loop	Expanding Your Sphere of Influence
Interview	Business Meeting
Asking for a Raise	Renegotiating a Contract
A big fan of outbound marketing	A big fan of inbound marketing
Job Description	Request For Proposal (RFP)
Believes in traditional Outbound Marketing	Becoming familiar with inbound Marketing

---

3.7 Let's Review Your Business Departments

The Business Model for the CEO of ME, Inc.

If you're catching onto the CEO of ME, Inc. paradigm, then you're beginning to see that YOU are the product your company "manufactures"; as such, you'll need to regularly analyze your strengths, weaknesses, and life/career values. What's more important, if you really *are* the product, you must be able to communicate the value and benefits you offer to would-be consumers (decision-makers).

Now if the approach is making sense, then the following chart listing your ME, Inc. "business departments" will provide an even deeper perspective. The graphic following the chart represents my attempt to introduce the paradigm visually to those who are not familiar with it:

Business Department	Description
Personal Board of Directors	Family, Extended Family, etc...
Research & Development	Networking Assessing Market Demand Research Methodologies Target Organizations Identify the "Hidden Job Market"
Sales & Marketing	The Job Description, Value Proposition, Interview Collaborating with Recruiters & Executive Search Firms Interviewing styles and formats
Communications	(same)
Business Development	Alternate sources of income
Legal	(same)
Accounting & Bookkeeping	(same)
Public Relations	(same)
Community Relations	Reciprocity, giving back to community
Channel Partner	Alternate sources of income
Training & Development	Investment in ME, Inc. Education, Certification, Mentoring Retention of Coach Board of Advisors
Technology	All technology impacting ME, Inc. LinkedIn, Indeed, Manta Blogging, ETP Network Toolbar Discussion Groups JibberJobber (relationship management)

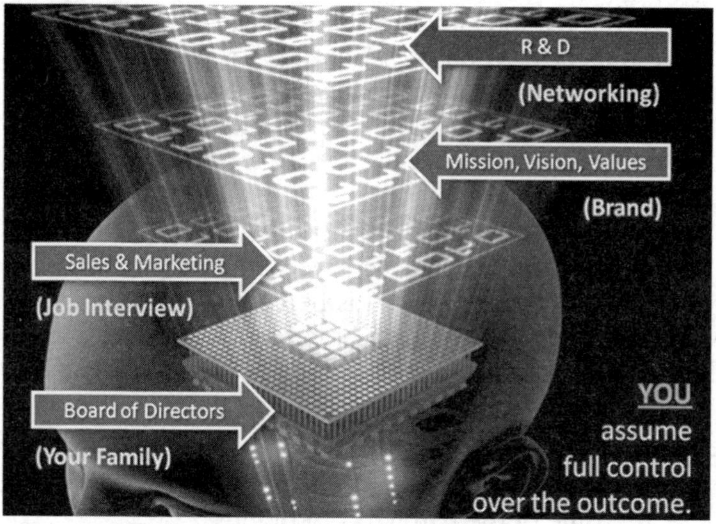
R & D
(Networking)
Mission, Vision, Values
(Brand)
Sales & Marketing
(Job Interview)
Board of Directors
(Your Family)
YOU
assume
full control
over the outcome.

3.8 Think, Speak and Act Like a Business Owner

The Business Owner Persona
In taking on the persona of a business owner, you need to adopt the attitudes, values, and guiding principles of a business owner. Anything less is insufficient.

Examples:

- Get used to handling rejection.
  It happens every business day.
- Learn how to manage risk.
- Make smart, calculated decisions.
- It's your move. Whatever you decide to do, you're responsible.
- Use the ETP Network to help evaluate individual risk.

- Develop a CEO mind-set so you can create a "business-to-business" entity.
- Run your career as a business.
- Build and leverage your network from a CEO's perspective.

The Personal Branding and Marketing of ME, Inc.
The total relationship people have with you gives them a certain perception of you. This perception is your brand. As the CEO of ME, Inc., your brand helps others decide if they **want** a relationship with you or not. (Learn more about Personal Branding in Chapter 12, *Break Away From the Pack*).

Here are some of the hallmarks of brands:

- You only get "credit" for what you do consistently.
- The reliability of your behavior establishes your brand.
- Brands are based on actions, not intentions.
- Inconsistency weakens brands and suspends belief.

This is how your brand will affect your job search:

- It establishes your value.
- It establishes trust.
- You consistently deliver value, therefore ...
- *You can negotiate!*

Remember this important marketing principle: **Benefits Always Trump Features.** *If a new car dealer tells you about 8 cylinder engines, state-of-the-art emission controls, moon roof, and racing stripes, she's describing the car's **features**. However, if she tells you things like, "It will easily save you over 50% on gasoline", or "the front and rear sensors warn you if you are too close to another vehicle", she's describing the car's **benefits** to you as the potential owner.*

Since you are the CEO of ME, Inc., always try to emphasize how you can solve someone's problem or save them money rather than going on and on about all the achievements you've racked up in your professional career. If people begin to associate you with consistently providing benefits, **that will become part of your BRAND — and you'll be remembered for it!**

Benefits Always Trump Features.

Remember this phrase when we get to Chapter 4, The Magnet: Your Value Proposition and Chapter 5, The Methodology: The 7-Step Job Search Methodology. When you learn how to prepare a powerful, targeted resume and cover letter, you'll want to reflect on this phrase because more than any single aspect of your resume, **demonstrating benefits makes you GOLDEN.**

Learn to differentiate yourself from your competitors. Always provide value. Bring something to the table they can't. Find a niche that shows the world you are someone with unique skills and talents **and that you know how to use them!**

3.9   Summary and Scoreboard

You've just read Chapter 3. In winning the race for 21st century jobs, you now know the following:

- Adopting the CEO of ME, Inc. mind-set allows you to run your career as a business
- There are striking differences between the ETP Network and The Black Hole approaches to the job search
- There should be a distinctive "breakout" of your

business structure showing the relationship between different components of your job search (e.g., R &D is networking, etc...).

	CORE CHAPTERS										
1	2	3	4	5	6	7	8	9	10	11	12
▲	▲	▲									

You now have three options:

1. Ignore the rest of the book and move on to other things.
2. Slide back into the dead-end comfort of The Black Hole.
3. Move on to Chapter 4 to learn about the ETP Network Value Proposition: what it is, why you need it, and how to put one together that will "wow" *any* hiring manager or decision-maker.

It's Your Decision.

Chapter 4

The Magnet: Your Value Proposition

4.1 Attract the Employer to You

What if there was a way to make yourself so appealing and attractive to would–be employers that they actually fought over you, phoning you day and night, begging you to come in for an interview or maybe even suggesting that you skip the interview process altogether? What if there was a way to make your name synonymous with "industry expert" or "saves companies billions of dollars every quarter"?

The concept is fascinating, isn't it? ... getting employers to come to *you*, expressing a need for *your* core skills, wanting to hear more about *your* background — even suggesting that *they call you* for an interview!

It sounds impossible. And in the race for 21st century jobs, it is. But the good news is that you can get tantalizingly close to that *type* of marketing dynamic by doing the following:

- Make sure that the position you're applying for is a *70% match* in terms of required core skills.

- Write a powerfully targeted resume that zeroes in on *meticulously vetted core skills* as listed in the company's job description.

- Write an equally powerful cover letter with logic, clarity, focus and relevance.

This chapter is all about "selling yourself"— making a solid, bulletproof case for your unique suitability for a particular position. The case I'm referring to is called a **value proposition.** Within the ETP network, a value proposition consists of three documents:

1. A **job description** for which you are unquestionably qualified and in which you are highly interested.

2. A **targeted resume,** i.e., a generic resume engineered to display experience "bullets" that are dead–on matches with the core skills specified within the job description.

3. A **targeted cover letter** (called a "T–Letter") that sum-marizes your perfect match–up in a visually succinct and easily scannable one–page document.

If the position described in the job description has been well-vetted, (i.e., it really exists, the core skills are clearly identified, and you are a dead-on match for those core skills) a first rate value proposition will hand decision-makers an interesting dilemma: **How can they possibly deny you an interview?** Based on my "insider knowledge" and years of experience, they can't. If the three compo-nents of your value proposition sing in perfect harmony, *an interview is yours.*

To do this, the guiding principle that must tick inside your brain every moment of every day is this:

- A solid value proposition helps me to land the interview.

- The interview helps me to land the job.

4.2   Grasping the Concept of a Value Proposition

It's interesting to watch courtroom programs like "Judge Jennifer" or "Judge Fred" in which a TV announcer first summarizes a plaintiff's case, then provides a similar narrative for the defendant.

Right from the start, we're exposed to the drama of courtroom conflict. We know that one of the litigants will prevail and that the other will not. In the mind of the judge, the difference between the two arguments will be based on which litigant presents the most credible and convincing evidence.

So let me ask you a question: Right now, if you had to make your "case" for a particular job, how convincing would it be? Is it rock solid, compelling, and bullet-proof? Or is it a limp pile of linguini that's not even sure it belongs on the dinner table?

If you're serious about getting a job you've identified, you'll need to take the information in this chapter very seriously. Here, I lay out the plan for you to develop your own *customized* value proposition. *It should come as no surprise to learn that your value proposition will become the key criterion by which a decision–maker determines your fitness for an interview.*

Before we go any further, let's make some distinctions.
In the business world, a value proposition is a statement of the benefits a client or customer receives as a result of doing business with you. *A value proposition is most effective when it offers specific, credible and verifiable evidence of your claims.* More than anything else, it must convey the value and benefits a product or service promises in a uniquely convincing way.

The reason weak value propositions fail is that they never actually address the key questions running through the potential employer's mind: "What can you do for me?" or "How can you improve my bottom line?" or "What can you do to help me increase market share?" From the decision-maker's perspective, *the very best candidates make a bulletproof case that the value they bring to the table is greater than the cost of hiring them.*

4.3   Build Your Qualifications Magnet

But Understand the Old Employment Model First
Decades ago, people could get jobs by simply submitting a strong resume and performing reasonably well during an interview. Jobs were plentiful, companies were recruiting heavily to attract good talent, and there seemed to be no end of wiggle room when discussing salaries, bonuses and perks. It was a *job–seeker's paradise* because of what it represented: You could be a cookie–cutter replica of everyone

else in line for the position and *still* have a great shot at getting a job—maybe not *the* job, but *a* job.

Now Understand the New Employment Model

The old employment model is gone. It's been replaced in the 21st century with what might be called the *Differentiate or Die* model. It goes like this: Unless you can convince the decision-maker that you are the one, truly, uniquely qualified candidate, there will be no interview, no "foot in the door." And that means no job. **Game over.**

Many years ago, companies had 5–year plans; today, everything is based on quarters. Businesses have much shorter attention spans than they used to. Very few organizations offer comprehensive training programs because it's more economical to let people go and hire new talent to replace them.

There is no single villain in this 21st century career management melodrama. Instead, there is an entire cast of shady characters, each of which contributes to an atmosphere of intense competition including the shortage of available jobs, global economic pressures, corporate downsizing, rapid turnover, increased demand for a highly specialized workforce, and so on.

The bottom line is this. If you can't distinguish yourself from the pack in a way that screams *"Value! Relevance! Direct Benefit!"*, your chances for landing the position are slim. On the other hand, if you brand yourself well and "live your brand" every day, you can create a **perception of value** and be considered someone who is truly "best in class."

As far as I'm concerned, the only way to achieve this status and stand out from others applying for the same position is to develop a rock-solid *value proposition*. The value proposition gives you an unusually strong competitive edge. Its purpose is to attract the decision-maker to *your* dossier above all others. Your paperwork must clearly differentiate you as someone with unique, relevant, high value-added talents and skills.

"But Do I Really Need a Value Proposition?"
Sorry — I just can't resist: This is kind of like asking, "Gee ... Do I really need a helmet when I go rock-climbing?" or "Do I really need to re-check my parachute? My 5-year-old said she already checked it for me."

I think I've made my point.

Yes, you *absolutely must* develop a value proposition for each position you intend to pursue. **Think of it as an insurance policy against mediocrity.**

You need a value proposition because it provides a platform from which to announce your outstanding qualities to decision-makers; because hundreds of other individuals will have skipped this critical step or at least not prepared one as bulletproof as yours; because you should attempt to gain tactical advantages over your competitors whenever possible; and because you need — and want — to attract and hold the roving eyes of decision-makers who are all too eager to glance at *other* resumes sitting on their desks, the resumes belonging to your competitors!

It helps to think of the value proposition as a qualifications magnet.

Now, for a moment, put yourself in the position of a decision-maker. You've got two candidates who've submitted paperwork for "Position X." One has a beautifully formatted generic resume that reads like a long drawn out testimonial of his or her most cherished accomplishments. The other is a tightly worded targeted resume with a perfect match–up of business qualifications (within the critical 3 – 5 year time period) for all of the core skills in the job description. And it has a perfectly integrated high–impact cover letter (T–Letter) to boot.

Which one will get your immediate attention? This is the power and attractive force of the value proposition. That's why you must develop one for **each** position you intend to pursue.

My friends, learn this lesson:

Let's say you're the owner of a neighbor-hood ice cream parlor. One hot summer night, a customer walks in and asks for two half-gallons of Peanut Butter & Prune Swirl Deluxe and instead you hand him a pint of Pistachio Mushroom Surprise. Is he going to be pleased? No. Instead, he'll go to the ice cream parlor across the street and get exactly what he wants.

Does it sound like a lot of work? It is. But think about the likely outcome if you back down and choose the low road instead, the "easy–out" option: Cutting corners on a value proposition is somewhat like building a house with balsa wood because it's lighter and cheaper. Will you get a house? Sure. Will it be cheap? Absolutely. Will it serve the primary need of providing comfort and shelter for you and your loved ones? No chance.

Common Problems
Many business owners make two key mistakes when writing their value propositions, particularly the "targeted resume." These key mistakes are:

1. Forgetting the most fundamental marketing principle: Always **emphasize the benefits** (value) you can provide **instead of the features** you offer. Features matter very little to those in a position to hire, purchase, or offer a contract; it's the direct benefits you can provide (e.g., increasing revenues, bringing a product or service to market faster, decreasing costs, improving operational efficiency, increasing market share, etc.) that matter most — that and your ability to do what you say you can do.

2. Going overboard citing your own *previous but irrelevant business experience*. This is a common resume error, usually due to your need to pat yourself on the back and *not* because this experience is relevant to the client or hiring manager's needs.

Know Your Core Skills Well
I will remind you of this often, especially in Chapter 5, *The Methodology: The 7–Step Job Search Methodology*. But it will also be highly instructive right now. *Before you actually learn to construct a value proposition*, you need to understand why a precise inventory of your core skills is essential.

Building your value proposition ensures that your core skills are a solid match with the core skills identified in the job description in which you're interested. As a general rule, you should be about a 70% or better match.

If you determine that the match is a good one, then this position is "in play" for you. If the match comes in at less than 70%, you need to reassess the job market to find a position where the skills are a better fit.

This alternate position may not be the niche of preference, but it's still a step forward in terms of securing income. In a case like this, it's important to "follow the money" and accept something a bit less than what you had hoped for while keeping your eyes and ears peeled for new opportunities. It's important to understand, as the CEO of ME, Inc., that this is not an admission of defeat, but a tactical short-term solution for running your business.

4.4 What is the ETP Network Value Proposition?

The ETP Network bases its job search methodology on the above sound marketing principles to help you develop and perfect a tight value proposition.

Within the ETP Network, however, the term *value proposition* has an even more precise meaning. It is the combination of three documents:

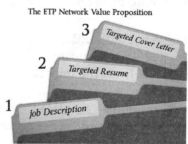

The ETP Network Value Proposition

1. **Job Description**
   (Are you thinking like a CEO? This is the RFP, Request For Proposal.)
2. **Targeted Resume** (Still thinking like a CEO? This is the client proposal.)
3. **Cover Letter,** or T−Letter (Got it? Good. This is your executive summary.)

It is this combination of documents that conveys the true value you hold for a potential employer and I will show you how to create targeted resumes and cover letters for maximum impact. You will use the job description solely for the purpose of creating the other two documents.

Here's how:

The ETP Network *value proposition* requires you to isolate a job opportunity whose "core skill" requirements are a strong match for your own. You will then craft a targeted resume in which you address each point (core skill) within that job description to show how, preferably in the last 3 – 5 years, you have demonstrated **verifiable experience** in that area.

Once the targeted resume is complete, you'll draft a cover letter, most likely a special kind of cover letter known as a "T–Letter." T–Letters are designed to compare the stated core skills from the company's job description against your proven experience for that skill. You'll write qualification statements as "responses" to each requirement statement. Each qualification bullet you write must answer the following questions:

1. What did I do?
2. For what company?
3. What was the impact?

When you've completed the value proposition, review it for strengths and weaknesses. If you've built a strong case, you should begin preparation for the interview.

Keep Your Eyes on the Prize
Picture two pieces of a jigsaw puzzle that snap into place perfectly. Let's consider the piece on the left the company whose position attracted you in the first place (along

with all of its stated core requirements). Now let's consider you and your relevant experience as the piece on the right. This represents the "perfect match" scenario, admittedly a rather rare occurrence in today's job market.

The real prize, however, is the far more realistic *70% or better* match scenario. The closer you can get to making your verifiable core skills match up with the core skills in a job description, the better your chances of getting called for an interview.

4.5   The Job Description

Mention the term "job description" and you'll probably get a chorus of "...*BORRRRRING!!*" in response. Yes, job descriptions are almost inconceivably boring. **But as CEOs managing a business, we know they are crucial to our success.**

The job description is your first clue as to whether a particular position is a good fit for you or not. If you can adequately match your skills to those required in a particular job description, then this document becomes the "trigger" for developing a value proposition. In fact, you won't be able to create a value proposition **without** one.

Ultimately, the job description is where you begin building your case for the job.

What is the Role of a Job Description?
The job description:

   • Provides a clear description of the job requirements

- Clarifies the employer's expectations for the employee
- Provides the basis for measuring job performance
- Prevents arbitrary interpretations of role content and limits by the employee, the employer and the manager
- Functions as an essential reference tool in issues of employee/employer dispute
- Provides neutral and objective reference points for appraisals, performance reviews and counseling

You'll need to train yourself to read job descriptions with a keen analytical eye. This way, not one scrap of skill information or experience will escape your attention. You'll demonstrate to decision–makers that you've got everything they're looking for and the best part of all is that **you can prove it!**

Because all the methodology I'll show you in Chapter 5 is built on an accurate interpretation of the job description, I recently introduced a kind of *mantra* within the ETP Network which goes like this:

"OWN THE JOB DESCRIPTION!"

Understand each word, phrase, acronym, idiom and nuance so well that an interviewer will be left speechless when he/she hears your command of the requirements. In fact, take it a step farther if you truly want all cylinders firing in your favor: *KNOW THE JOB DESCRIPTION BETTER THAN THE INTERVIEWER!*

This is one of the most powerful and disarming techniques a candidate can exploit. It will easily catch interviewers off–guard, swinging the pendulum of conversational advantage back to you — the candidate — which is exactly where you want it.

4.6 Generic Resumes

Not only have you seen them, you probably have one: a generic resume. It's the document you pull out of the file cabinet when someone tells you about a position that may be interesting ... but it's light on **relevant** details (or doesn't supply them at all). It over—itemizes extraneous work experience, sharing details that might impress your family and friends but not a decision—maker looking for relevance.

Generic resumes are exactly what the name implies: non—specific, "baseline" resumes that describe your skills, list professional experience, and provide supplemental information like education, contact information, etc. You would be horrified to learn how many people actually submit generic resumes when applying for a position they've isolated with my 7—Step Job Search Methodology. It's appalling. Can you imagine a hiring manager who scans a resume for a position that has clearly defined core skills, only to see a grossly **non—targeted resume** with absolutely **NO** relevance?

If this is something you've done recently, you may have unwittingly given yourself two black eyes. But you're the CEO of a business: Learn the lesson and move on.

Does this mean generic resumes have no value? No. They're good starting points for developing targeted resumes. When you identify a well—matched position, you can use your generic resume as a point of reference from which to build the targeted version.

4.7 Targeted Resumes (TRs)

As a fifteen–year veteran of Human Resources recruiting in both a corporate and an agency setting, I've devoted a third of my life to reviewing resumes. During this time, I saw every combination of resume fads and styles. It is abundantly clear to me that professionals spend too much time and money developing a winning resume **when the client is not looking for a resume at all.**

The client is not *really* interested in a full accounting of your education and employment. What he or she wants to know is if you have the required skills for the job and if you've successfully demonstrated mastery of those skills, preferably within the last 3 – 5 years.

Here are the questions most likely to be running through the client's mind:

- Does the candidate have the required skills?
- Does the candidate clearly describe how he/she used the skills in his/her last few positions?
- Does the candidate demonstrate success in the skill sets required?
- Does the candidate have enough of the skills to be worth pursuing even if he/she is not a perfect fit?
- Is the candidate able to clearly communicate this on the resume or is it poorly written?
- Are the compensation expectations in line with the role?
- Is the candidate a fit from a "level" (grade) perspective? Is he/she looking to take a major step down just to find employment and then leave once a better opportunity presents itself?

- What is the risk in hiring the candidate?
- Will the candidate fit within the culture of the organization?

Most decision-makers review a countless number of resumes each day. **On average** you only have 10 - 15 seconds in which to make a powerful first impression. If your "TR" doesn't "grab them" right away, there may not be another opportunity to grab them at all.

Still more food for thought: In the race for 21st century jobs, we are now living in an age of **consensus hiring** — the decision of "yea" or "nay" is not up to just one individual but rather a whole team. Your ability to "connect" with the entire team matters a great deal.

Finally, you'll have a much better chance of being considered for an interview if the experience you cite is relevant, current, and clearly written. This way, no one with input on your suitability will misunderstand or misinterpret what you've written. **That is the power of the targeted resume.**

Separating Resume Fallacies From Facts

Fallacy

- The purpose of a resume is to list all your skills and abilities.
- A good resume will get you the job you want.
- Your resume will be read carefully and thoroughly by an interested employer.
- The more good information you provide about yourself in your resume, the better.
- If you want a really good resume, have it prepared by a resume service.

Fact

- The purpose of a resume is to spark employer interest and generate an interview.
- All a resume can do is get you in the door.
- Your resume probably has less than 10 seconds to make an impression.
- Too much information on a resume may kill the reader's appetite to know more.
- *Resumes are written to impress, not inform. Think of your resume as a marketing tool, not an historical record. It is valuable real estate, so use it for your most impressive but relevant information.*

Specific Steps for Preparing a Targeted Resume:

1. Copy and paste the core requirements and responsibilities from the job description into a blank document.
2. Place a bullet "•" before each key requirement/responsibility.
3. You now have a list of key questions the client/company will ask you on the interview.
4. Now put the list in priority order — here, you must try to think and act as if you are the decision-maker to determine priority.
5. Select the top 5 to 8 skills from the list and write below each one how you have accomplished the requirement/responsibility including the impact/result of your work.
6. You now have the content to build both a great targeted resume and your talking points for the interview.
7. Incorporate your answers into the generic resume and you now have the beginnings of a powerful targeted resume.
8. Delete/remove from your resume facts/details that have no value for the job.

4.8   The Cover Letter (T-Letter)

There are many formats to choose from when drafting a cover letter. Many people prefer a straightforward, para-graph–based cover letter simply because they're comfort-able with it or possibly because they haven't heard of other, possibly better formats.

The T–Letter
One style in particular that we in the ETP Network find exceptionally beneficial is the **T–Letter.**

The express purpose of a T–Letter is to demonstrate — with strong visual impact — exactly why you are uniquely qualified for the position you seek. If you've done your homework well and selected a position for which you are a dead–on match, a T–Letter gives you the chance to lay out your case for the job "point by point" using a chart in the middle of the letter. The chart compares each core requirement for the job on the left with a corresponding "qualification bullet" on the right demonstrating how you have proven experience for that requirement.

WARNING!
Don't even THINK about developing a T–Letter BEFORE you've written your targeted resume. The T–Letter is developed only AFTER the targeted resume has been completed and verified for accuracy.

T–Letter Layout (Greatly Simplified)

Your Name
Address
City, State, Zip Code
Phone Number
February 25, 2009

Ms. Jane Doe, Title
Ajax Lugnut Corporation
555 Pine Street
Duluth, MN 55555

Dear Ms. Doe:

I am very interested in the position of Administrative Assistant listed
in the Daily Tribune on February 24, 2009. The skills and qualifications
you mention closely match my experience in this career field.

Your Needs	My Qualifications
• Detail–oriented, experienced Administrative Assistant	• Four years Administrative Assistant experience with responsibility for numerous detailed reports
• Assist Customer Relations Manager	• Assisted Customer Relations Manager for two years Regularly served purchasing agents at Fortune 500 companies
• Corporate experience with major clients a must PC knowledge a plus	• Hands–on experience with Lotus 1–2–3 and WordPerfect on IBM–PC

Enclosed is my resume for your review and consideration. I believe
I am an excellent candidate for this position and look forward to
meeting with you to discuss it in greater detail. I will plan to call you
to determine when an interview might be possible. Thank you.

Sincerely,

(*Signature*)
Typed Name

Steps in Building a T-Letter

1. Read and analyze the job description for the position of interest.

   > Look for the *core requirements* of the job, then decide if your skills — especially those you've used within the last five years — are a 70% or better match.

2. If you have not yet developed your targeted resume for the position, stop working on the T-Letter now. The T-Letter is written only **after** you have a knock-'em-dead targeted resume first.

3. If you have already written your knock-'em-dead targeted resume, proceed with the T-Letter.

4. In developing a good T-Letter, think in terms of the "4 L's": **Layout, Logic, Linkage, and Language.**

   • **The Layout:**
   The layout is the format of the letter itself (see previous example). It has the date, your contact information, an appropriate salutation, an opening paragraph, the "T-Display" block in which you compare your qualifications (on the right) against the job description's stated core requirements (on the left).

   • **The Logic:**
   This is where you'll build your case for the position. The stronger your qualification statements, the greater your chances of being advanced to an interview.

Important: Each qualification bullet must answer 3 questions:

1. What did you do?
2. Where did you do it?
   (company / business / organization)
3. What was the impact?

- **The Linkage:**
  Earlier, we said that the three components of a value proposition (job description, cover letter, targeted resume) must "sing in perfect harmony" to resonate with decision–makers. There is no room for inconsistencies, contradictions, or failure to synchronize the documents perfectly. You must **engineer** error–free linkage between the targeted resume and the T–Letter.

- **The Language:**
  Use powerful, non–abused action verbs; avoid "corp speak" and double–talk. Make your qualification bullets brief but filled with impact. Strive to make them sound unique. The way you write your T–Letter is not necessarily how the decision-maker will read it, so be extra careful about phraseology, syntax, grammar, punctuation, etc...

4.9 Your Interview Attraction Machine

If you've been diligent in applying the tips and techniques described in this chapter for the assembly of your value proposition, then what you've just built is a wonderfully efficient *interview-attraction machine.*

You have built a rock-solid case for being advanced to an interview well ahead of everyone else in the pack — especially those who are still unaware of the ETP Network and its commitment to helping professionals in transition land as quickly and safely as possible.

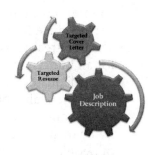

You've built your case and you've built it methodically and powerfully. It's a case that can't be ignored for one very simple reason: It's bulletproof with regard to relevance and quality. Even decision-makers who only scan resumes for ten seconds won't be able to put yours down ... and why should they? They've just found their perfect candidate: *You!*

With your newly developed interview-attraction machine, you're ready to tackle the 7-Step Job Search Methodology.

Congratulations!

4.10   Summary and Scoreboard

You've just read Chapter 4. In winning the race for 21st century jobs, you now know the following:

- When each component of your value proposition MESHES PERFECTLY with the other two, you have a POWERFUL value proposition.
- The targeted resume and the T−Letter help you get

an interview; but it's the interview – and your performance in it – that actually gets you the job.
- The only real reason a company will not call you for an interview is that you haven't built your case adequately.
- Your case (value proposition) must be written clearly, since many individuals will review it. Why? We are living in an age of consensus hiring in which teams of people – not just one individual – review your application.

	CORE CHAPTERS										
1	2	3	4	5	6	7	8	9	10	11	12
▲	▲	▲	▲								

You now have three options:

1. Ignore the rest of the book and move on to other things.
2. Slide back into the dead-end comfort of The Black Hole.
3. Move on to Chapter 5 to learn about the centerpiece of the entire book, my 7-Step Job Search Methodology.

It's Your Decision.

Chapter 5

The Methodology: The 7-Step Job Search Methodology

5.1 Seven Steps That Could Change Your Life

For those of you who purchased this book **today** thinking that you'd skip directly to this chapter, read it, and get a job **tomorrow,** I have one thing to say: **Good Luck!**

And if you somehow manage to pull that off, I'll nominate myself for a Pulitzer *the minute you sign your contract!*

Enough!
Pour yourself a cup of coffee and let's get to work.

This chapter presents my **7-Step Job Search Methodology.** It is a procedure that's been tweaked to near-perfection over the past five years but will undoubtedly be tweaked many more times whenever improvements are discovered, tested, and evaluated.

As you step yourself through this process, we'll take the networking skills you learned in Chapter 2, the powerful CEO mind set from Chapter 3, and the magnetic attraction of your value proposition from Chapter 4 and weld them together for maximum impact.

To do this, your CEO business brain must think in four dimensions, i.e., remember that each component (networking, CEO mind-set, value proposition, and methodology) becomes **supercharged** when combined with the other three but has ample horsepower to stand on its own when the situation calls for it.

This will be challenging work and at times you may become frustrated. But the payoff is substantial: *You will cut yourself free from the grip of The Black Hole.* Instead of being dependent on *people who don't know you* to advance your career goals, you will learn to **network your way** to an interview, job or contract by leveraging the power of **advocates** — *people who not only know you, but like you, trust you and will gladly help you to "connect the dots."*

5.2 Decision Time: Do It Right or Don't Do It at All

The 7-Step Job Search Methodology comes with a few caveats. *Please make sure you understand them because each has a critical purpose. The omission of any one of them may nullify your best efforts.*

- This is a 7-Step Methodology. Not four. Not six— *Seven.*

- You must execute all seven steps for the methodology to work. If you skip a step, the methodology will **not** work. If you forget a step, same result.

- Think of the methodology as a giant loop: When you reach Step 7, you must go back and start the process all over. Do not expect to achieve success by stepping yourself through the procedure a few times, getting discouraged, then abandoning the effort. **Keep working the process.** There is momentum and magic in the repetition.

- You need to make a genuine effort to understand each step. You must say to yourself, "What's going on here? What is Rod *really* asking me to do?" You can take your chances on following the steps blindly, but if you're not sure *why* you're doing them, what good can they serve?

    *Note: I've provided **reasons** and **rationale** for each step along the way. If you don't understand why a particular step is necessary, please join the ETP Network and ask your questions during our regularly scheduled programs, events, and webinars.*

- The "7 Steps" are listed in sequence. Do Number 1 first. Do Number 3 third, and so on. Arbitrarily changing the sequence renders the methodology useless.

- You cannot afford to be indecisive. At various points in the methodology, you'll need to make tough decisions. **Make them!** You're the CEO of a business!

- The "7-Steps" provides **strong probability** — but **no guarantees.** There is a far greater chance of finding a job with this system than through The Black Hole.

- Thoroughly familiarize yourself with the use of **LinkedIn.** It is an integral part of the procedure. If you think you'll need assistance with *LinkedIn,* please find a good reference or browse through some online bookstores.

5.3 Preparation

I have prepared a *learning sequence* that will help you absorb the methodology as efficiently as possible.

- **First,** I'm going to give you a high level overview of the "7 Steps" in plain English. Don't be concerned if the terminology is unfamiliar; just try to get "the big picture." (Section 5.4)

- **Second,** I'm going to present the detailed procedure of the "7 Steps" in the same way that ETP Network members learn it: a) the procedure; b) the tools; c) the business rationale for doing each step; and d) helpful notes, tips, suggestions, possible pitfalls. (Section 5.5)

- **Third,** I'm going to present an illustrative walkthrough of the "7 Steps" for an ETP Network member so that you can visualize how you might carry out the procedure for your own situation. (Section 5.6)

- **Fourth,** I'll provide you with an analysis of the illustrative walk-through to give you an idea what, if any, mistakes were made. (Section 5.7)

- **Last**, I'll provide some Frequently Asked Questions that are typically asked by those who first learn this methodology. (Section 5.10)

To get started, you'll need an updated **generic resume** that can be used as a template for creating your **targeted resume.**

5.4   Seven Steps: High Level Overview

Step 1
First, you will determine what *your* core skills are. Everyone is good at something; so what are *your* skills, talents, and abilities? What would be a suitable title for someone who does your kind of work?

Step 2
You call your work by a particular name; now it's time to find out what the *marketplace* calls it. Are you a Java Developer? A Financial Analyst? You'll make good use of a web site called *Indeed.com* to perform this task. You'll also get a first look at opportunities that may be a good fit for you. The importance of this step is that it helps you determine the *market demand* for your skills (i.e., the *spot market;* a snapshot of what the *prevailing* market conditions look like).

Step 3
Now, using *LinkedIn* and your networking skills, try to identify advocates; these are people either in your network or in the networks of friends, business contacts, etc... who can "connect the dots" for you within a targeted company to get your name circulated among key decision-makers. At this step, you are performing "networking research", that is, you are not actually reaching out to these advocates yet, just identifying who they are and adding their names to a list of potential advocates for the perpsective company.

Step 4

You will then develop your **value proposition** consisting of: 1) a targeted resume; 2) a cover letter (or T-Letter), and 3) the job description itself. In this step you are building your case for the job. Since these documents will either make or break you, you will want to have them as close to perfection as possible.

> *Note: Although the value proposition consists of 1) the job description, 2) the targeted resume, and 3) the T-Letter, you will only actually submit the resume and cover letter. Decision-makers don't need to see the job description. We include it as part of the value proposition to make sure that we keep ourselves properly tracked with its requirements while engaging advocates.*

Step 5

Once you're SURE you understand the position for which you've identified suitable advocates, prepare to connect with them. For advocates who are in a decision-making role, you'll place a call to them and **sell,** i.e., your "Sales & Marketing Team" swings into gear. With advocates who are friends, or friends of friends, you'll network to establish a communications chain to the decision makers (your "Research & Development Team" manages this) and insight to how best approach and navigate within the company. **In all cases, you will document all contact with advocates to ensure timely and appropriate follow-up.**

Step 6

After that, you will submit your value proposition as instructed and set up a specific follow-up schedule. You will track your contact with all advocates to ensure that no follow-up calls or e-mails are forgotten.

Step 7
Finally, you will repeat the process. As the CEO of a business, you never settle for having just one client. When you're in transition and actively looking for work, your goal should be to find at least one new client per day.

5.5 Seven Steps: Detailed Procedures

STEP 1:

IDENTIFY THE CORE SKILLS YOU PROVIDE TO A CLIENT OR A COMPANY

PROCEDURE
1. *Examine your generic resume.*
2. *Review the core words (skills) that stand out; highlight those words.*
3. *Try to identify 3 – 5 core skills.*

TOOLS
- *Generic resume*
- *Highlighter*

BENEFITS / BUSINESS RATIONALE
- *All CEOs know their company's products and services. How can you be in business otherwise?*

NOTES

Make sure your generic resume is current in all areas.

STEP 2:

IDENTIFY MARKET DEMAND FOR YOUR CORE SKILLS

PROCEDURE
1. *Get your list of 3 – 5 core skills ready.*
2. *Run the "Advanced Search" on Indeed.com to filter positions you find.*
3. *You have a 70% match (your skills measured against an available position) when you can answer "yes" to these three questions:*
   a) *Can I do it?*
   b) *Can I prove it?*
   c) *Am I interested?*
4. *Print the job opening and save it electronically for use in Step 4.*

TOOLS
- *Indeed.com* (www.indeed.com) – Advanced Search feature

BENEFITS / BUSINESS RATIONALE
- Think of the job description as a *Request For Proposal (RFP)*
- You're not really in business until you find a client; you must identify the **market demand** for your core skills.
- CEOs make informed decisions and rely heavily on business intelligence they gather through their R & D Departments. They also keep current on technology and hold themselves accountable for mastering certain online applications that can have a direct impact on the company's bottom line.
- As a business owner, would you ever "skim through" an RFP? Then why would you skim through a job description?

NOTES
- If there is NO market demand, go back to Step 1 and zero in on different skills.
- Make sure you have a good handle on the appropriate key words and titles that match what you do. Consider getting advice from a career coach. The reason for filtering the results in *Indeed.com's Advanced Search* is to get more qualified (more precisely targeted) opportunities.
- Using *Indeed.com* at this step helps you to determine **market demand** (the "spot market"; a snapshot of what the **prevailing** market conditions look like).

STEP 3:

IDENTIFY POTENTIAL ADVOCATES

PROCEDURE: GROUP "A" ADVOCATES
Create a list of potential decision-makers, that is, those with decision-making authority who currently work at a targeted company or agency in human resources or talent acquisition.

PROCEDURE: GROUP "B" ADVOCATES
Using LinkedIn, find individuals working at the company who may have some knowledge of the job opening or who can potentially assist you to navigate inside the organization. Your goal is to seek the Group "B" advocate's wisdom and guidance as to the best approach navigating inside the company.

TOOLS
LinkedIn (www.linkedin.com)
Advocate worksheet (available to members)

BENEFITS / BUSINESS RATIONALE
- By doing this, you tap relationships, mentors, and decision-makers directly and indirectly. In so doing, you remove yourself from The Black Hole.

- Throughout Step 3, you are using the R & D Team and Sales & Marketing Team of your business. Like any great CEO, you're using business intelligence so you don't leave anything to chance.
- There is a "traceable path" from you to an advocate and beyond.

NOTES
- Who are "decision-makers"? Recruiters, Staffing, Recruitment, HR, Human Resources, Talent Acquisition, etc... are your Group "A" Advocates.
- Group "B" Advocates are individuals who potentially have access to decision-makers or provide you with guidance inside the company.
- You should attempt to find suitable advocates within 48 hours of locating an appropriate job opportunity.
- IMPORTANT: For Group "A" Advocates, you will always make a **direct call**. Why? They are hired by the organization to bring in the best talent. E-mail just doesn't cut it.
- Group "B" Advocates **must** work at the target company. They can be friends, or "friends of friends", or even "friends of friends of friends." (Here is where you will begin to really appreciate the **role of the connector** as we discussed back in Chapter 2!). Phone scripts are available for both Group "A" and Group "B" Advocates.
- When connecting with advocates, remember: **Always follow up!**
- Do not settle for finding just one advocate. We never "single-thread" our way into an organization; we always "multi-thread."
- Your goal is to find one Group "A" Advocate who is willing to work with you and find 5 to 10 Group "B" Advocates inside the company who are willing to assist you in some capacity.

STEP 4:

PREPARE VALUE PROPOSITION: TARGETED RESUME PLUS COVER LETTER

PROCEDURE

1. *Prepare your targeted resume:*

   a) Copy & paste the job description's core requirements and responsibilities into a blank file (you prepared it in Step 2).

   b) Answer the questions posed in viewing the core requirements, responsibilities (i.e., what are they looking for? – answer in bullet point format).

   c) Answer the questions with the following format: What did you do? Where did you do it? What was the impact?

   d) The answers for the questions above should be written based specifically on the last 3 – 5 years of experience.

   e) Incorporate bullets into generic resume; you now have a targeted resume.

2. *Prepare your cover letter (T-Letter)*

   a) ETP Network members can refer to the document called"The Executive Summary: A Job Aid" to prepare a T-Letter.

   b) All necessary steps are contained in that document.

3. **Keep the original job description with the targeted resume and cover letter.**

TOOLS
- Generic resume
- Well-matched job description
- Cover letter job aid

BENEFITS / BUSINESS RATIONALE
- Throughout Step 4, you will be *building* your case for the position (*not making it; that comes later*).

- The targeted resume you will produce should be thought of as your proposal.

NOTES
- The stronger and more compelling your case, the easier the upcoming step (Step 5) will be.
- Caution: Do not attempt to write a cover letter (T-Letter) unless you have completed your targeted resume and verfied that it is *properly* targeted.
- Your targeted resume plus an appropriate cover letter plus the job description (RFP) constitutes your **value proposition.**
- In the ETP Network, we strive to understand each selected job description as thoroughly as possible. **We strive to "own the job description" in order to gain a tactical advantage during the interview.**
- Writing a properly targeted resume is challenging: You must resist the temptation to supply an exhaustive list of all your accomplishments stretching back far beyond the period of relevance.
- If you don't properly target your resume, it will make finding advocates far more difficult: Why? Because as "connectors", they will not want to put their reputation on the line for someone who is providing them with a weak or lackluster value proposition.
- Be wary of your resume writer: If you hire someone to write your resume, remember that you're entrusting them with the most important task that separates you from the position you want. They may be excellent at crafting a beautiful looking document, but if it's not properly targeted, isn't compelling, and doesn't really make your case, what good is it?

STEP 5:

CONNECT WITH THE ADVOCATES YOU IDENTIFIED IN STEP 3

PROCEDURE

1. *Group "A":*
   a) *Prepare your 40-second sales pitch. Refer to Group "A" Advocate Phone Script (available to members)*
   b) *After 48 hours, leave a voice mail and follow up every five (5) business days.*

2. *Group "B":*
   a) *Reach out to "Connector # 1" to reach a Group "B" Advocate.*
   b) *Reach out to "Connector #2" (if needed).*

TOOLS
- *LinkedIn*
- Targeted resume
- Cover letter (T-Letter)
- Phone Scripts for Group "A" Advocates (available to members)
- Email Scripts for Group "B" Advocates (available to members)

BENEFITS / BUSINESS RATIONALE
- Now that you're armed with your business case, you're ready to **make** your case.
- We need "cheerleaders" (Group 'B" Advocates) to help us pick up the human factor, i.e., recommendations, testimonials, shared experiences.

NOTES
- Make sure your phone scripts and email scripts are strong and convincing.
- When Reaching out to Connectors, make sure to provide them your Value Proposition in order to help them connect you to Group "B" Advocates.

STEP 6:

SUBMIT AND FOLLOW UP

PROCEDURE
1. *Submit paperwork as instructed/advised by advocates.*
2. *Follow up as indicated per conversation with advocate.*

TOOLS
- Value proposition (for submission)
- Advocate worksheet for follow-up (available to members)

BENEFITS / BUSINESS RATIONALE
- We're now in the business aspect (solicitation); we're submitting our proposal to the client based on **their RFP!**

NOTES
- Quality is critical at this stage.
- Failure to follow up can ruin the entire effort. Don't let it happen.

STEP 7:

REPEAT THE PROCESS

PROCEDURE
Go back to Step 1. This is an ongoing, cyclical process.

TOOLS
This book and/or a Job Aid called "The 7 Steps" (available to members)

BENEFITS / BUSINESS RATIONALE
- No client is guaranteed a "yes" on each submission.
- Attitude throughout the job search is key:
  If you can't convince yourself that you're a good fit for the position, how do you expect to convince anyone else?

NOTES
- Never let five (5) business days pass without a follow-up telephone call or email.
- Why build a network and then never use it? Some people make the mistake of preparing top-notch documentation but then fail to send it to someone in the network; this is indicative of someone whose thinking is still stuck *inside* The Black Hole.
- A word about **quotas** (attention: Sales & Marketing Team)... How many leads are you generating per week? As a business owner, we don't just settle for one lead a week. *At a minimum, we strive to find one lead per day and six per week. This helps to keep the search momentum going strong.*

5.6 Seven Steps: Illustrative Walk-Through

Kristen McAllister is a graphic artist and page layout specialist based in Austin, Texas. She was employed as a computer graphics specialist at **West Texas Wildlife Magazine.** *While there, she also contributed articles to this glossy, full-color monthly magazine with a circulation of about 200,000.*

As the magazine began to cut staff, Kristen sensed that her job was in jeopardy. As an ETP Network member who believes in the principle "Never Stop Networking Even After You Land", she started notifying her network that her "job status was changing." Ironically, only a few days later, she got a pink slip. Here is what she did:

Step 1
Referring to her generic resume, she made a list of her strongest skills; in her case, the list included computer graphics, illustration, page layout, and copywriting.

Step 2
In order to find the market demand for her skills, she went online to Indeed.com and entered "computer graphics" as one of her core skills along with her zip code; this gave her a rough idea of what opportunities were available within a 25-mile radius of her home. Using Indeed's Advanced Search feature, she further filtered the information to isolate certain types of jobs, or locations, or distances from home. Based on the results, she found six opportunities within 25 miles of her home for a computer specialist.

Step 3
Because she believes strongly in the power of networking, Kristen immediately began researching her contact list and her LinkedIn connections to find advocates at one particular company, the **MacPherson Design Group.** She found three advocates who were connected to her as either Level 1, Level 2, or Level 3 on LinkedIn. In addition, she was able to find a 3rd level connection who works in the HR Department at **MDG.** She made good use of the ETP Network's telephone scripts.

Step 4
Since she now had her advocates lined up and had an excellent understanding of MDG's core requirements from their posted job description, she began developing her targeted resume. She did this by eliminating all of the irrelevant bullet points from the experience section of her generic resume and moved her relevant experience from the past

3 – 5 years into the first group of bullets. In this way, she was assured that a hiring manager would see that she was qualified for the position at first glance. For added insurance, she carefully built a cover letter (a "T-Letter") and included all of her relevant experience bullets matched one for one against the stated core requirements. She knew that a decision-maker would be able to glance at her T-Letter and tell in an instant that she was qualified. Her goal was to remove all doubt from the decision-maker's mind.

Step 5
Since she took great care in identifying advocates in Step 3, she now consulted the ETP Network "phone scripts" (for reaching out to hiring managers, HR, recruiters, etc...) and her "email scripts" (for reaching out to individuals who could act as proponents within MDG). She knew that a solid connection with even one advocate would be helpful, but she also knew that it is always better to "multi-thread" into an organization than to "single-thread." The more connections that are working for you, the greater your chances are of reaching the goal: getting the interview.

Step 6
With the connection to a "decision maker" at MDG, Kristen put the finishing touches on her targeted resume and her T-Letter. Per instructions from a Mr. Kimball in HR, she submitted her paperwork and asked when she would be notified about the call for the interview. She negotiated a follow-up schedule to ensure that her hard work would not be lost or overlooked. About two weeks after submitting her paperwork, she was called for an interview at MDG. After several rounds of interviews, she was notified by an MDG HR Manager that the company selected her as the best candidate and made her an offer.

Step 7
Kristen reported for work at MDG. New job landed! Success! Job Search completed.

5.7   Seven Steps: Analysis

Overall, Kristen did a good job in applying the 7-Step Methodology — after all, she **did** land a new job. Her application of the methodology was mostly sound. Nevertheless, there are a few points to highlight:

- In Step 2, while using *Indeed.com*, Kristen needs to be careful about "grabbing" a position just because it's filtered by *Indeed.com* and looks appealing. What she really needs to do is this: For each position identified, she must ask herself three *qualifying ques tions: 1) "Can I do it?" 2) "Can I prove it?" 3) "Do I want it?"* If the answer to all three questions is 'yes', she's ready to move on to Step 3. If not, she needs to restart the methodology at Step 1.

- Kristen needs to use an Advocate worksheet to track all contacts with advocates. This ensures that follow-up is carried out in a timely manner, increases her appearance of professionalism, and keeps her "front and center" in the minds of the decision-makers.

- As a quality check in Step 4, Kristen needs to reconsider how well her targeted resume and T-Letter pair up. If they fail to complement each other or appear even slightly mismatched, that's enough to ruin her chances for an interview.

- Kristen must not fall into the trap of thinking that because she landed safely she can now abandon her networking efforts. In fact if she has truly absorbed the methodology, she understands that getting the job is only part of the overall process; the other part is being vigilant for new openings.

The business rationale here is that no business is ever satisfied with having just one client; businesses are always on the lookout for new customers. As the CEO of ME, Inc. she is a business. Even after landing, her R & D and Sales & Marketing teams must remain busy. In this way, when the next downsizing occurs, her "safety net" is already built; it's strong, flexible, and ready to be mobilized as she requires.

5.8 What You Need to Remember About Advocates

There are two categories of advocates that will help you land your next position.

> **1. Group "A" Advocates** *are the* <u>stakeholders</u> *in the candidacy and hiring process, i.e., the decision-makers. Be prepared to deploy your Sales & Marketing Team to interact with Group "A" advocates (i.e., selling).*

> **2. Group "B" Advocates,** *by contrast, are* <u>cheerleaders and personal advisors</u>*. Be prepared to deploy your Research & Development Team to interact with Group "B" advocates (i.e., networking).*

Understanding this difference between these two groups is important because your questions, interactions and relationships will differ significantly from group to group.

It works like this. Once you've identified a position you're interested in and for which you are a solid match, you need to identify your Group "A" advocates before submitting your value proposition.

The best source for finding Group "A" advocates is *LinkedIn*. When performing a search for these advocates use the following helpful keywords: *Sourcing, Talent, HR, Human Resources, Recruiter, Staffing, and Procurement.*

If you don't find advocates on *LinkedIn* there are many other searchable sources such as the company's web site, *Manta*, and numerous social networking sites. Also don't forget your offline network which may consist of family, friends, neighbors and acquaintances who may have connections at the target company.

In addition, it's important to find Group "B" advocates at the target company since these people can help you understand the best way to position your skills, talents and experience. Since every corporation has its own culture and processes, business intelligence is the most effective way to navigate the system of gatekeepers. In fact, accurate information is invaluable. I've known qualified candidates that were great matches for positions, but they missed out on opportunities because they didn't present their skills in the proper manner for the target company. You need to speak their language — after all, isn't that what a targeted resume is all about?

Once you've identified both Group "A" and Group "B" advocates for a position, you'll be armed with the information and support system that allows you to manage the hiring process for maximum effect.

Finally, regardless of the outcome of your job search process, remember that your advocates have exerted time and effort in assisting you so be sure to thank them appropriately and in a timely manner!

> **"Things are beginning to make much more sense now ..."**
>
> *In the Introduction to this book, I made a large fuss over the "connectionless environment" of The Black Hole. Recall that the primary reason The Black Hole can't deliver results is that there are no human-to-human connections, just interactions with online forms and an assortment of computers.*
>
> *Now, however, you can finally see the "connected environment" at work within the 7-Step Job Search Methodology. By **networking** your way to decision-makers via **advocates,** you tap the power of your relationships to reach the people who can help you get the position or win the new client.*
>
> **Reaching your objective is now firmly under your control because you have built a warm, trusted network of trusted relationships — with living, breathing, caring and compassionate human beings!**

5.9   Seven Steps: Frequently Asked Questions

Question # 1 – Jennifer S., Allentown, PA

"Rod, doesn't this whole process seem like an awful lot of work just to find a new job? In The Black Hole, I'm done within 5 minutes. Your methodology looks as if it could take weeks, maybe even months!"

Answer # 1

Yes, it is a lot of work. But didn't you agree to view your job search as a business back in Chapter 3? Are you going to abandon that mind-set so quickly? Business owners work hard to achieve their goals; as the CEO of ME, Inc., why shouldn't you?

NEWSFLASH: That "5 minutes" you spend in The Black Hole doesn't include weeks of waiting for an answer. And guess what? In some cases, the answer **never** *comes — remember that you're not interacting with live communicating people, just a bunch of computers. In terms of human interaction, it is a totally* **connectionless** *environment.*

Do you **really** *expect "quick" results from a connectionless environment?*

Question # 2 – Carlos D., Lincoln Park, NJ
"Why do I have to call Advocates in Group "A" as opposed to e-mailing them which is so much faster?"

Answer # 2

It's not as impactful. You need to sell your value proposition and nothing beats talking with an advocate directly. E-mail may be faster for you, but it may get far less attention on the receiving end, a scenario you clearly want to avoid.

Question # 3 – Linda C., Tampa, FL
"Why do I have to recreate a resume when I have a template for a core work skill?"

Answer # 3

The issue is we're running a business. We don't deal with generic information. We need to be able to influence the decision-maker to a "yes" decision, right? A generic resume doesn't really address any *specific needs. Your proposal must address what the client is looking for and then really **nail** it. We call it a targeted resume.*

Question # 4 – Mark A., Lakewood, NJ
"How often do I follow up with an advocate?"

Answer # 4

Roughly once a week, according to the Keith Ferrazzi follow-up model we use. *To be effective, every follow-up gets an e-mail **and** a voice mail. Both must be very positive in tone and be sure to reiterate your interest. If you have a discussion with an advocate in Group "A" and/or "B", they're going to give you an estimate of when you can expect to hear back ... that's when you need to say something like the following: "If I don't hear back from you by {date}, may I call you back on {date + 1}?"*

Question # 5 – Danielle R., Mendham, NJ
"Do I rely on one advocate in an organization as a cheerleader (Group "B")?"

Answer # 5
We want as many cheerleaders as possible. Just remember the comparison to a real cheerleader: If you're playing football, do you want to hear just one cheerleader in a stadium or a whole squad of cheerleaders stirring up the whole crowd? It's the same principle here.

Question # 6 – David C., Stroudsburg, PA
"Do I tell an advocate about my work with other advocatesin the organizations?"

Answer # 6
Yes, as long as the advocate is going to do something for you. But if he or she is just gathering intelligence for personal use, then

*there's no need to share information. As a courtesy, it's always better to **try** to let them know.*

Question # 7 – Adelaida D., Princeton, NJ
"How do I find a phone number for a company?"

Answer # 7
First, go to the company website. If you can't find the information there, use Manta.com or any other web site where corporate information is provided (e.g., Hoovers.com).

Question # 8 – Charlie M., Atlantic City, NJ
"What is an Advocate Worksheet?"

Answer # 8
An advocate worksheet is a spreadsheet that mirrors the 7-Step Job Search Methodology. It allows you to track every client advocate with details such as dates of contact, comments shared, agreed-upon follow-up dates and times, notes of special interest, etc. ... Its primary purpose is to ENSURE that you follow up with an advocate.

Question # 9 – Isaac T., Verona, NJ
"How do I find a job if nothing shows up on *Indeed*?"

Answer # 9
There are several possibilities here. First, you may have an incorrect job title; check your bio, your resume, and any targeted resumes you've written. Select titles that are appropriate for what you've actually accomplished. If you still have a problem, seek out the counsel and wisdom of individuals with whom you've worked in the past to help you identify "core titles."

Question # 10 – Nikki B., Charlotte, NC

"Is there another way of finding a job other than *Indeed.com?*"

Answer # 10

There are hundreds of job search engines that are available. Alternatives are Dice, Monster, NetTemps, etc. We have a toolbar (built by COO Carl Reid) with a "smart radar" system that allows qualified users to get "feeds" of opportunities that are relevant to their specific search criteria.

Question # 11 – Jacqueline S., New Rochelle, NY

"I hate using the Internet to find a job but that is what you're asking me to do. Isn't there any other way?"

Answer # 11

In business, as a business owner, we often have to do things we don't like to do. Market demand (a key component of the 7-Step Methodology) is much more efficiently displayed and analyzed using the Internet. I have two suggestions for you:

- *Try to get comfortable with the Internet; it's not going away any time soon.*

- *Make sure you read Chapter 11, The Awesome Power of Attitude and Behavior; it sounds like yours could use a tune-up.*

Question # 12 – Jason K., Los Angeles, CA

"I don't want to work in my core area of expertise – what do I do?"

Answer # 12

*First of all, what is it you **want** to do? If you're running a business, you have to know what products and services you offer. What have you done? What skills are transferable and what are they transferable to? Once you know, find mentors who know people that hire people like you. Determine market demand. You might also need some training, so keep this option open. Invest time connecting with individuals who are currently in the new industry you want to join.*

Question # 13 – Maricel M., New Brunswick, NJ
"I don't have anyone at Level 1 (*LinkedIn*) who can help. What should I do?"

Answer # 13

LinkedIn is a great contact database and it's always good to have a solid base of Level 1 connections. I'm sure you can find friends and business associates (current or former) who would be glad to hook up with you. And don't forget: Once you get those Level 1 connections, the real power of LinkedIn is not in how many Level 1 connections you have; it's in the extraordinarily broad reach of your Level 2 and Level 3 connections. In fact most people who actually land jobs through the assistance of LinkedIn connections get those jobs via Level 2s and 3s, not Level 1s.

Question # 14 – Della S., Greensboro, NC
"What if I don't really know what I want to do?"

Answer # 14

Find people who are doing something you consider "pretty cool." If your reaction is, "I could do that!", then you may have just identified an area you can explore.

Question # 15 – Maria C., Portsmouth, OH

"How many job opportunities should I be trying to find each week?"

Answer # 15

Here's the best "rule of thumb": **Find one opening a day!** *The reason? It keeps momentum going and keeps your attitude positive. Never let a day go by without finding at least one opening. Success or failure lies in finding one opening a day.*

Question # 16 – Sam R., Denville, NJ

"Rod, this is not directly about the 7-Step Methodology, it's about the connection process and the requirement for a valid value proposition before you connect someone with someone else. Why do you insist on a value proposition just to connect someone? Lots of other people in *LinkedIn* simply hook people up and that's that. What's the big deal?"

Answer # 16

Good question, Sam. Before I answer it, make sure you understand the way I'm using the term 'value proposition' as it applies to network connections: It's not the three documents described in Chapter 4; that's the "case" you build for a position you've already targeted.

Instead, the value proposition — in terms of connections — is simply the answer to this question: "What value do you have that will benefit the person you want me to connect you to?" If the answer is "none", then I don't feel comfortable about making the connection because that puts me (as the connector) at risk. I suggest you re-read that section titled "Protect the Connector" in Chapter 2.

Finally, let me add this: Building a ME, Inc. business requires you to accept the responsibility and accountability for your mission/vision/value in running ME, Inc. You cannot rely on the old premise that you are "owed something" or carry any kind of entitlement mentality.

ETP is not looking for professionals sitting around in a circle holding hands and singing "Kumbaya." We need professionals to feel great about being the CEO of ME, Inc. — the individual they see in the mirror — **YOU.**

5.10   Summary and Scoreboard

You've just read Chapter 5. In winning the race for 21st century jobs, you now know the following:

- The job search will be a piece of cake as long **as your skills are in demand within the market you're going after !!!**
- On the targeted resume, make sure you give clients what **they're looking for**, not what **you** want to share.
- A top-notch value proposition is the key to getting the interview; the interview is the key to getting the job.
- Any employer will hire any individual as long as the employer is convinced that hiring him or her will bring more value than it costs.

CORE CHAPTERS											
1	2	3	4	5	6	7	8	9	10	11	12
▲	▲	▲	▲	▲							

You now have three options:

1. Ignore the rest of the book and move on to other things.
2. Slide back into the dead-end comfort of The Black Hole.
3. Move on to Chapter 6 to learn about *The Hidden Job Market*, an expansive reservoir of jobs that are out there and up for grabs — except that many aren't advertised and some don't even exist until you create them yourself!

It's Your Decision.

Chapter 6
The Hidden Job Market

6.1 Hiding in Plain Sight — Almost

Have you ever seen a painting in which an artist has blended two completely different images onto a single canvas? You stare at the canvas, clearly seeing a lion's head. But stare a little longer and the lion's head morphs into a herd of zebra grazing on the savanna. The zebras were there all along, just hidden until your eyes reprocessed the scene.

The same is true of the 21st century jobscape. Of course there are the usual, regularly-posted jobs on *Indeed.com* and other search engines; but another layer of opportunities exists — not immediately visible — and definitely not posted! We refer to this unseen layer as the "Hidden Job Market."

Many new job seekers are surprised to learn that there is such a thing as the "Hidden Job Market." "After all," they say, "Why should an available job **not** be posted along with all the others? Maybe my dream job is out there somewhere and I won't even get a chance to review the job description!"

Unfortunately, that's not a tough-as-nails CEO speaking but a whiny little 3rd grader who just got kicked in the shins during recess. You need to switch your thinking from *child-like complaint mode* to *business intelligence research mode* for your own good, the good of your business, and the good of your Personal Board of Directors.

6.2   What is the Hidden Job Market?

The Hidden Job Market is the name given to all the opportunities out there that are unadvertised, either because a company wants to find candidates through its employees' networks or because no such position currently exists. In the last case, you must depend on your own ingenuity to identify *potential opportunities* at an intriguing company, do your homework to determine what that company truly needs, then figure out how to create an attractive, value-added position. Finally, you need to "sell the concept".

How Do You Access It?
Due to the sheer volume of applicants competing for a fixed number of positions, many employers don't even bother registering their openings on big-name job boards like *Monster*, *Dice*, and *CareerBuilder*.

Instead, they turn to their existing employee network to help recruit qualified candidates. This means there may be great opportunities at a company of interest, but you'll never find out about them via the traditional approach of querying Internet job boards.

Why would an employer do this? There are two immediate advantages. First, hiring managers can avoid the torrent of paperwork from job seekers who aren't even remotely qualified for a position. Second, they can bypass the registration process with the job boards and confine interview time to a bare minimum.

There's something else you need to know about the Hidden Job Market. Step 2 of the 7-Step Job Search Methodology (Chapter 5), is based on the **spot market.** In other words, it uses today's market conditions to determine what positions are currently available. By contrast, the Hidden Job Market is based on the **futures market,** that is, the **potential** for positions that might exist or that could be created in the future — your future.

6.3 The Role of Networking in *the Hidden Job Market*

You've built a network of trusted relationships. But why bother to network if you never plan to leverage it? **It's now time to do some asking because you've earned the right to do so.** You've followed the rules and observed the connection protocols. It's time to tap your network's **connection horsepower** to help you find a position.

In order to set you up with the proper mind-set for exploring the Hidden Job Market, I'd like you to consider the following somewhat offbeat illustrative scenario:

Let's say you're a surgeon who has been assigned the task of finding and removing a dangerous tumor somewhere in the lower abdomen of a 52-year-old man. Theoretically, you could start performing exploratory surgery right away, reaching in through various incisions to feel for any lumps or masses.

But is that really a medically sound practice? Before performing surgery, wouldn't it be better to gather as much information about the soft tissue in the patient with a CT-Scan or an MRI? Wouldn't these diagnostic procedures give you far greater intelligence about size, shape, and precise location of the tumor? And wouldn't it make much more sense to have all of the diagnostic work completed before the first incision is ever made?

The point is this: **While investigating the Hidden Job Market, your primary function will be networking, not selling, and your aim is to gather intelligence from those individuals in your core skills space.** Your job is to connect with individuals who can truly help you because they're in the same industry, not going on some fishing expedition inside industries that have no relevance to yours.

To put it in slightly different terms, it's not going to do you any good to tap into a pipeline of business intelligence for the pharmaceutical industry if you're seeking a position in the financial services industry. You need to refine the "filtering" of your contacts to make sure you're picking up intelligence for the industry — and, if possible, even the precise niche — in which you want to work.

Your ultimate goal is to answer two very specific questions:

1. *Who does what you do?*
2. *Who hires people who do what you do?*

Once you've mastered this "precision targeting" technique, the flow of your conversation will be along these lines:

"Where do you see the industry heading? What's going on? What's hot? What's not? What groups should I belong to? This is what I'm hearing; what are you hearing?"

Finally, when you judge it to be the correct time to do some asking, you must do it as an assertive CEO, not a spineless wimp. It must be a direct request for a specific action to achieve a targeted goal. Don't worry, you've earned the right to ask because of your golden reciprocity track record. Furthermore, most business owners appreciate direct, straightforward requests.

6.4 Uncovering *the Hidden Job Market*

The first step in uncovering the Hidden Job Market is to thoroughly research your target employer. Discover where you can provide a useful service or offer money-making or money-saving ideas. Then present your qualifications for the job or service so convincingly that the employer can't resist creating a job for you.

Finding opportunities that aren't posted requires a combination of ingenuity and diligence. If you're good at digging up information and gathering business intelligence from normal networking activities, you should be able to get promising results from the Hidden Job Market.

Here are some specific suggestions:

- Expand your search tools (don't confine yourself to one job search engine; there are several out there and results can vary significantly).

- Do **Google** searches on keywords associated with your industry to bring up names of organizations, memberships, employee directories, etc... Again, they don't pop up out of nowhere; you need to be diligent and persistent.

- **Craigslist** is a potential source of leads that can fall through the filter of Internet job boards. There are documented incidents of job seekers finding their "perfect job" by combing through *Craigslist* postings every day.

- One of the very best sources of information about companies and contacts within companies is our old friend, **LinkedIn.** Continue to use *LinkedIn* to gather information about people, companies, trends, innovations, mergers, reorganizations, major announcements, etc.

- An excellent way to ferret out a company's "inside intelligence" is to tap into its online network through the power of social media sites like **Facebook** and **Twitter.** If you tend to dismiss these sites as "gossip centers", you're making a mistake. Businesses are leveraging the power of rapid information exchange to stay ahead of the curve on trends and issues affecting their industry. *Many postings on these sites are gold mines of industry-specific or niche-specific information.*

- One of the great lessons learned from Keith Ferrazzi's book <u>Never Eat Alone</u> is that job seekers must learn to be ***bold and audacious.*** In that vein, there's no law against picking up the telephone and contacting a company directly with suggestions about how your products or services will bolster their bottom line.

- Blogging is another great source of leads into companies of interest. How? Visit a company's blog and post some insightful comments. If you leave a link back to your own blog, you can easily start picking up feedback streams of replies from employees.

What it boils down to is this: the Hidden Job Market is created through your own ingenuity. But penetrating this market relies on the same machinery that drives all your "regular" job searches: **networking.** Let's take a look at the role of networking in reaching this somewhat elusive target.

6.5 Tapping Into Your Network for Job Leads

For the most part, employers base their hiring decisions on trust. They are more likely to hire people they know or those referred by people they know. For this reason, your warm trusted network is your No. 1 source of solid job leads.

Step	Action	Process
1	Define your job target so you can complete job search forms on recruitment sites	Identify keywords you can provide in keyword fields to produce job matches on recruitment sites. Identify your preferred geographical locations, employment industry, and salary range.
2	Research employers	Research employers' web sites.
3	Prepare a resume and cover letter	Prepare and transmit properly formatted resumes and cover letter tailored to each employer's needs, including targeted keywords.
4	Find online job listings	Check employers' web sites. Check job listing sites.
5	Apply online	Carefully follow the sites' job application instructions. Register or fill out the access screens on job listing sites Post your resume and cover letter as required by the sites. with your job target information (Step 1 above). Before submitting the final online application, print a copy for your files.
6	Follow up, if possible	Call the employer; indicate that you have applied online a for a specific job ad. If possible, contact the decision maker.

6.6   The Networking Process

Most networking professionals agree that network members are your strongest source of job leads. As such, they can form an excellent bridge to your perfect job if you follow the guidelines listed below. Following these suggestions in order will create maximum impact and yield best results:

1. **Make an appointment to meet in person.** Make appointments with the most viable of your networking members. Appointments get the best results. In each meeting, briefly review your job objective and ask for recommendations. Give each person a copy of your cover letter and resume, asking for feedback on the content and quality. Be organized and respect the individual's time.

2. **Make a telephone call.** If you can't arrange an appointment, make a telephone call. Briefly review your job objective and ask for recommendations. Ask whether you can send a copy of your cover letter and resume to get your contact's feedback.

3. **Send a networking letter.** If you can't arrange a meeting or reach the person by telephone, send a networking letter.

6.7 The Networking Letter

A networking letter tells your network about your job search goals and requests specific help with the process. It contains basic, core information and personalized comments tailored to the recipient. Want to skip this step? Don't even consider it: the employment success rate from networking letters is high.

Your networking letters should:

- have a friendly, enthusiastic, and confident tone
- use a professional format with no errors
- convey a complete, concise message that clearly identifies your job target and job search goals
- request specific help
- refer to your resume

Tailor your networking letters to the individual strengths of your network members. Ask a good writer for advice on improving your resume. Ask others to help you identify specific employers or direct job leads. You can also request meetings with some network members to brainstorm strategies.

6.8   Final Thoughts

The Hidden Job Market is comprised of jobs that are not advertised. Your mission in the Hidden Job Market is to uncover as many jobs as possible. Once you have identified a job, immediately go to Step-3 (Finding Advocates) of our 7-Step Job Search Methodology (Chapter 5) and follow the subsequent steps.

Think big! The Hidden Job Market is limited only by your imagination. You have nothing to lose and everything to gain by tapping it in your bid for an interview or even the creation of your own position!

6.9   Summary and Scoreboard

You've just read Chapter 6. In winning the race for 21st century jobs, you now know the following:

> There is an often-overlooked part of the job search landscape called the Hidden Job Market. You know how to make inquiries about jobs that don't yet exist but which might be created if you provide a compelling value proposition.

	CORE CHAPTERS										
1	2	3	4	5	6	7	8	9	10	11	12
▲	▲	▲	▲	▲	▲						

You now have three options:

1. Ignore the rest of the book and move on to other things.
2. Slide back into the dead-end comfort of The Black Hole.
3. Move on to Chapter 7 to learn how to manage the transition to a new position.

It's Your Decision.

Chapter 7

The Interview and Negotiations

7.1 Lights! Camera! Action!

Most of us have been in the spotlight at some point in our lives. Maybe we were the lead in a school play, a soloist in a church concert, or the valedictorian at commencement exercises. For many people, being in the spotlight is enjoyable and exhilarating. For others, it can be awkward and terrifying.

Up until now, all of the work you've done to find, target, and pursue an interesting position has been behind the scenes, with no need to actually polish your shoes in order to put your best foot forward. After all, who needs freshly polished shoes to write a targeted resume? Or a 3-piece suit to call some Group "A" Advocates? Unless you plan on meeting them in person, no one will ever know you're wearing faded jeans and a T-shirt.

That's why no aspect of the job search is as nerve-wracking as the interview. This is the time you must shine. Your suit must be perfect. Your smile must be perfect. Your nails must be perfect. The reason? Before you utter a single word you're being evaluated. Even though you are the CEO of your own business, you are nevertheless in "Sales and Marketing Mode" during the interview. Your appearance, demeanor, and body language will be carefully and silently scrutinized. The overall impression you give will speak volumes about you before you've had a chance to say "Hello."

That can mean only one thing:
It's time for some mental toughness!

With such intense pressure, it makes sense to prepare for the interview with the same discipline an engineer uses to construct a high-rise.

That preparation is the focus of this chapter. Here, we share tips that thousands of ETP Network members use to prepare for interviews and ultimately for victory in the race for 21st century jobs.

7.2   Own the Job Description

By now, this phrase should sound quite familiar. You heard it back in Chapter 4 when you developed your value proposition. Back then, I stressed the importance of "owning" the job description so you could create a value proposition with high impact.

If you can **truly** claim "ownership" of the job description, you're in an unbeatable position to navigate the interview. In fact it's a sure thing since you're already intimately familiar with every detail that could possibly emerge as a talking point.

Think of it as **curveball insurance;** If the interviewer attempts to throw you a curveball with some obscure reference to responsibilities or skills, you can respond with confidence and poise to demonstrate your unbelievable mastery of the position's unique requirements. Believe me, this makes a powerful impression!

7.3   Quick Tips for Interviewing

When I say quick, I mean it. The bulleted lists that follow include the best tips and suggestions I've found for managing the interview. No elaborate explanations are needed. All you need to know is that these tips work.

7.4   The Phone Interview

Your client is measuring you against their most critical needs including your:

- Technical skills
- Communication skills
- Energy
- Excitement

In other words, you have the technical skills; otherwise you would not have been selected for the interview. But while your competitors focus solely on this one attribute, your client is measuring *all four of these primary needs*. This is the perfect opportunity for you to clearly project your communications skills, your energy, and your excitement. It will give you a significant advantage over the competition.

Here are some specific tips that will position you well for the phone interview:

1. Make sure you're on a **_landline telephone_** during the interview. Landline phones project your voice more clearly than cordless phones, mobile phones, and Internet phones. If you have no choice but to use a mobile phone, make sure you have 4-5 bars of signal strength and that you are stationary during the call.

2. Make sure **_your voice is full of excitement and energy_**. Here's how:

   • Stand up. You will have better voice projection than your seated competitors.

   • Have your resume in front of you. Place each page side by side so you can easily see the entire document while you're listening and talking. Often, interviewers can hear the rustling of pages and they can sense any resulting disconti nuity. Your goal is to be as smooth and clear as possible when you deliver your information.

   • Face a mirror. What you see is what the inter viewer gets. When you smile, the interviewer knows it; when your competitors frown, the interviewer knows that, too. Many of your competitors may not realize that their facial expressions are discernable over the phone.

3. **Speak positive**, affirmative messages before the call and during the call.

4. **Maintain your enthusiasm, energy, and positive interest** in the position throughout the interview.

7.5 The Face-to-Face Interview

Often, the face-to-face meeting follows the phone interview. Now that you've intrigued them, your clients want a fuller understanding of who you are, what you can do for them, and how you'll fit in with their group.

These are the questions of greatest interest to them:

- Can you represent my team to the other groups?
- Can you represent the company?
- Do you fit into the organization?
- How are you going to interact with my team?
- Can you handle the particular intra-and
- inter-departmental dynamics, the culture?

Days or the Day before the Interview

It's necessary to do some homework to prepare for the interview. Here's how:

- Do a *Google* search on the company. Learn what they do, their type of business, their primary competitors, competing products and services, and so on.

- Do an additional *Google* search on the people you're interviewing with. Read the job description as if you were the author. Identify 4-5 key areas the client is most interested in. The key areas are usually at the front of the job description. Match 3-4 examples from your work experience with each of these key areas. Be prepared to answer questions during the interview but also to provide live examples of your success in each area. Explain how you can transfer that success to the new organization.

- Look your best. Make sure you carefully select and prepare your business attire. If you're not sure, there are many good books and web sites on the topic. You can also get input from your network or an image consultant.

- Print several copies of your resume, one for each interviewer. Have a nice pen, a pad of paper, maps, directions, and your business cards ready.

- Visit the site the day before the interview to ensure that you know the route, the traffic, the building, the parking, and the entrance.

Hours to Minutes before the Interview

- If you feel nervous or are having butterflies in your stomach, drink some lemon juice before the inter view. It's an old trick but it works.

- Pack your resumes, pens, paper, portfolio, business cards, maps, directions, etc. ahead of time so you don't forget anything and don't have to rush.

- Begin your commute early to ensure that you arrive at least 15 minutes before the interview.

- When you arrive, locate the rest room. Make sure that you are in proper shape (your hair is in order, no lipstick on the teeth, tie is straight, and so on).

- Wash your hands with warm water and soap. Dry your hands very well so that your hands feel dry, warm, and clean for the hand shake. The hand shake is very important. Before leaving the rest room, look at yourself, take at least 4 deep breaths and say "I will do great! I'm going to get the offer."

During the Interview

- Ask whether it's OK for you to take notes. If yes, take out a pen and pad.

- Be sure you have copies of your resume. Offer your clients each a copy. Do not put a copy of your resume in front of yourself. You should know your resume by heart.

- Lean forward; nod your head positively to show interest and affirmation at appropriate times.

- Maintain eye contact with the person who asks a question. Be aware that in a panel interview, you tend to look mostly at the person who smiles. Remember to look at the person who asks you the question instead and to periodically smile at others in the room.

- When given the opportunity to ask questions, focus on the following:

  - How does the company measure success?
  - How will you be measured by your manager?
  - How critical is your role?
  - Is there an incumbent?
  - What made the incumbent successful in the role?
  - What are the performance metrics used to measure success?

- DON'T ask questions about issues within the company or your potential career path. You will have opportunities to cover these later— after you receive the offer. In addition, don't get into every tiny detail about your new role. The interview is not about you, it's about them — what their needs are and how you can satisfy those needs.

- Finally, be sure to ask for their business cards and give them yours in return. If they don't offer, simply say, "May I have your business card?" If they give you an excuse for not reciprocating, they may be signaling that they don't want you to contact them — which is obviously not a good sign. By contrast, the exchange of cards usually means the dialogue will continue.

7.6 Negotiations

Negotiations are unique to each individual and to each individual client engagement. For every negotiation you undertake, maintain a CEO's mind-set with clarity and purpose as your goals. Ask yourself if this is a short-term gig or a long-term engagement. The answer is directly tied to the financial status of ME, Inc. Remember that this is a critical matter to your Personal Board of Directors. Depending on the situation (if you're currently unemployed your compensation is zero) you may have to settle for a client on a short-term basis while you continue to look for better mid-and long-term opportunities.

Other points about negotiations:

- This is a business to business discussion. You are a CEO so act accordingly.

- You are on equal footing with the client — provided you have a service the client is looking to engage.

- It's all about negotiating the details.

- Depending on the level of mutual interest, every offer has some wiggle room.

- Always ask "Is this your best offer?"

- Never say "no". Instead, offer a counter proposal that you are prepared to say "yes" to.

- If you're asked, it's OK to talk about money. If you're not asked, it's best to stick to the facts, then you can negotiate when you prove you're the best candidate for the job.

- When asked what salary you're looking for, reply "What are you budgeted for?" *Always counter with a follow-up proposal.*

- Ask your network for guidance prior to the negotiations. Seek anecdotal information on the organization's salary and benefits programs.

- Use *www.salary.com* to give you a baseline idea about salaries.

- Unless there are other reasons for you to move (e.g., industry, core competency expertise, location, etc.), you are seeking at least a 20% bump in salary.

- At times money may not be available but other

benefits can be negotiated (e.g., vacation, training, bonus projection, title, future movement, large projects, more responsibility, leadership within the organization or representing the organization externally to grow the network, tuition, association fees, etc.).

- You always have time to think about an offer; ask how much time you have and bring in your Personal Board of Directors to help you develop a great counterproposal.

- Saying "yes" doesn't mean you're getting married; it just means you are being engaged by a client to do "X" for a period of time. Your commitment to each other is mutually beneficial. When the engagement is no longer mutually beneficial the relationship should end. Stay ahead of this process instead of being caught off guard. Never forget that your real work is running the business of ME, Inc.

- Employers pay you what the position is valued at, not what you are worth. Don't take this personally, simply consider it vital information about how they see the role and its importance to the organization.

- One special key to negotiations is this: Early in the interview process, make a compelling, up-front argument as to why you are the best candidate for the job. The earlier and more compelling the argument, the better your negotiations will be.

- Never make the mistake of prematurely asking for money, benefits, or perks during the interview. Why? These issues are part of the negotiation process. Knowing the difference demonstrates your business savvy.

- Build a foolproof case for yourself so the interviewers don't find any weakness to hold against you.

- *"We're looking to bring you on board"* ... that's a signal ... so is *"how soon can you start?"* When the client makes the transition from being a buyer to wanting to be sold, change your responses accordingly.

- An ideal negotiation is a win-win. If you push the client into a corner to get an unrealistic salary, you'll be off to a bad start. Instead, both parties should feel that they gave up a little to get a lot. As the CEO of ME, Inc., this is a skill you must continuously sharpen.

7.7 Summary and Scoreboard

You've just read Chapter 7. In winning the race for 21st century jobs, you now know the following:

- You know how to prepare for the most nerve-wracking part of the job search: the interview. You've examined some practical tips to make your interview and negotiations run as smoothly as possible.

CORE CHAPTERS											
1	2	3	4	5	6	7	8	9	10	11	12
▲	▲	▲	▲	▲	▲	▲					

You now have three options:

1. Ignore the rest of the book and move on to other things.
2. Slide back into the dead-end comfort of The Black Hole.
3. Move on to Chapter 8, *Once You've Landed,* to find out why, as the CEO of ME Inc., your current job search ends once you've landed but your next job search begins as well.

It's Your Decision.

Chapter 8
Once You've Landed

8.1 You're Hired: Now What?

When we started discussing the CEO of ME, Inc. paradigm in Chapter 3, I playfully suggested that you "strap yourself in" because paradigm shifting can be a long and bumpy ride. Having said that, you may want to consider buckling up again as I explain what needs to be done after you've landed a targeted position. What I'm going to say will probably seem 180 degrees out of phase with what you'd expect.

Many people are stunned to learn that landing the long-sought after job is actually the **starting point** for their next job search. Let me repeat that for emphasis —
the starting point for their next job search!

Typical reactions from the *"newly landed"* include *"This is preposterous!"*, *"Why bother with all that networking when I don't have to?"*, and *"Why spend time gathering business intelligence if I've already landed a great job and I'm now getting some pretty nice paychecks?"* And let's not forget the most frequent response, *"Why endanger my performance on the new job by loading up my daily schedule with networking and job search stuff that's clearly not needed any longer?"*

What's that? Did I really hear you say *"job search stuff that's clearly not needed any longer?"* I thought so.

You don't really think you're going to be working for the *Purple Fudge Doughnut Emporium* for the next 20 years, do you? **Get with the program!** With rare exceptions, there are no more long-term assignments. In fact, one estimate of the average term of employment today is between two and four years — that's it.

Based on that statistic alone, you'll once again find yourself connectionless or at least connection-deficient if you take a vacation from networking, staying on top of the job market, and remaining tuned in to industry trends. Allow me to paint the picture for you: You'll be standing at the base of a very high and familiar-looking mountain looking straight up to its summit. And guess what? **You'll have to climb it all over again!**

The Right Approach

OK, now that you know the wrong approach, let's look at the right one.

Assuming that you found your new position as a result of *working* the 7-Step Job Search Methodology, you now have an unobstructed view of the business landscape both inside **and** outside of your new environment.

You have access to good, solid business intelligence relating to 1) the company for which you're working, 2) the industry in which it's niched, and 3) research gathered from tools like *Indeed.com*, *LinkedIn.com*, and Social Networking web sites (see Chapter 10, *Social Networking — Be A Part Of It*). Let's not forget to include 1) the fabulous information-sharing that goes on during ETP Network's networking events and 2) the regularly updated information from a wide range of business news web sites.

In addition, your new job allows you to gather a great deal of business intelligence simply by networking with your new co-workers. In today's environment, anyone who accepts a position at a company and fails to build connections, construct relationships, and gather business intelligence might as well be tossing a brick of pure gold off the Golden Gate Bridge.

How did we get to this place? Let's revisit the way business is trending in the 21st century: You already know the average life expectancy of today's jobs. So if you budget some networking and business intelligence-gathering time into your new schedule, you are (in effect) taking out an insurance policy on your next period of transition. Isn't it great to know that, within a reasonable amount of time, you can create a safety net of contacts at your new company plus contacts among that company's customers and suppliers? These contacts can then be 1) patched into your existing network, and 2) tapped when that next *pink slip* arrives.

If you're not convinced that this approach has tremendous value to a CEO running the business of ME, Inc., just imagine the day you get your next pink slip — and how much worse it will feel if you've *done **nothing** to extend your network!* Talk about feeling lonely and isolated! At that point, you may even be tempted to crawl back into The Black Hole just to feel "plugged in", at least at some primitive level, anyway.

8.2   The First 90 Days

During your first few months in a new position, you will obviously want to manage your workload carefully, but downtime provides good opportunities for the following activities, all of which are intended to shore you up when your next job loss occurs:

- Network actively with your new fellow employees (i.e., build and expand the "safety net").

- Manage your new relationships; nurture them with the idea that they will lead you to others and in all cases, connect with them on *LinkedIn*.

- Check *Indeed.com* regularly to see what kinds of opportunities are out there even though you are temporarily secure.

- Explore the "Hidden Job Market" to gather business intelligence, discover market conditions, spot trends in your industry, and so on.

Here is what you need to understand about the first few months in your new job. I'm presenting it as it was shared with me during a training conference call by a member who not only mastered the methodology, mindset, networking machinery and value proposition but who also understood the extraordinary value of keeping those processes going **after** he landed his new position.

In the words of ETP Network Leader Tom Kenny:

"The first 90 days are all about securing the first year. In any new position, it's important, as CEOs, not just to meet expectations, but to exceed expectations.

But if I abandon my networking activities just because I've landed, I'm taking myself out of the very loop that got me here in the first place: my trusted contacts in the Warm, Trusted Network. It took me a long time to build that net-

work; why would I want to let go of it now, especially when most business and economic trends show that a majority of people will go through a job search roughly once every three years? What if I have to re-engage my network unexpectedly?

*Naturally no one should give their new responsibilities a lower priority than networking. But all of this has to be put in perspective: Most of us, in the course of a business day, have at least **some** free time, time to just rest and recharge the batteries. That free time can still be thoroughly enjoyable if you meet some people in the cafeteria and share information, ideas, and opinions. You're still networking, it's just that you're assigning it a different 'rotation' in your business day."*

There's another point to consider, and it's important. Even after being hired by your target company, you are still (and will remain) the CEO of ME, Inc. In that life-long position, you must not relinquish the duties of managing your career. You don't STOP being the CEO of ME, Inc. just because you've accepted a position and now have a new title. Your real title remains — the CEO of ME, Inc. The only real difference will be how well you strike a balance between managing your new client's responsibilities and the overarching responsibilities for your CEO of ME, Inc. enterprise.

8.3   Where the Focus Needs to Be

Here are the guidelines I believe will help you as you begin your tenure at your new position:

1. Focus on these three goals to help you
    adjust successfully:

a) Keep a positive attitude;

b) Project a professional, competent image; and

c) Be a good team player.

2. Learn about the company and culture, work efficiently, be dependable, focus on people, and prepare for evaluation.

3. Be a good communicator, manage yourself, build a network, and demonstrate maturity.

4. Be a high-quality, top producer and a problem solver; learn to adapt to and manage change, be flexible.

5. Take on new challenges, broaden your skills and knowledge, seek a mentor, develop expertise, keep your portfolio current, network constantly, and increase your visibility.

6. Keep your job search network active and maintain your ME, Inc. business model (the ETP Network's five core goals):

a) Secure a job/business where passion and income intersect

b) Build a trusted personal network of 200+ people

c) Create a career backup plan

d) Generate multiple sources of income (not in conflict with the primary source)

e) Become a networking leader

8.4   Dig Your Well Before You Need the Water

This timeless axiom perfectly describes the mess you'll be in once you've cycled through the 7-Step Job Search Methodology, gotten the interview, received the job offer, accepted it, and started working at the target company **without** nourishing, expanding, and regularly pinging your network.

For many, the problem is **complacency.** Once you've ended those horrible months of waiting for just the right position **and then you get it,** the tendency is to think like this:

> *"Well, I worked hard. Very hard. It was a long, uphill battle, but I fought my way to the top and now I've landed. I'm so exhausted now that the only thing I can think of is digging into my new work assignment. I don't have time for networking anymore; I need to refocus my priorities, and the priority right now is getting paychecks again."*

Does this sound familiar? It's all too easy to lapse into complacency. But if you do, it can have the effect of sabotaging all of your previous networking efforts or at the very least cause you to have very little to show for them.

How do you handle that?

Many ETP Network members simply schedule some periodic networking time during their new work week — even if it's just a few minutes here and there to make some phone calls, meet someone for lunch, or reconnect via e-mail. When you're newly employed, it doesn't take much effort to keep your network "alive", but whatever that effort is, it must be on a regular basis — something you consistently integrate into your weekly routine.

8.5   Did Someone Say "Advocate"?

For Those Who Forgot ...
A few scant chapters ago you were hooking up with Group "A" and Group "B" advocates, the human stepping stones needed to get your face and value proposition in front of key decision makers. Remember how great it was to have these people helping you?

So let me ask you something: Now that you're employed at the *Ajax Lug Nut Consortium*, are you going to shut out everyone who supported **you** during your arduous search? Are you going to chuck the ETP Network's mutual support philosophy just because some hard work finally led you to a safe landing? I hope not.

If anyone reading this says "Hey, wait a minute! *I'm OK now;* why should I get tangled up trying to help others? Look, I'm busy!" — then you might be what's known as a *"Closet Networking Leech (CNL)"*.   None of us suspected you were a "CNL" when we shared the weekly conference call microphone with you. You sounded sincere and compassionate. Just as we pledged to be there for you, we believed you would be there for us during *our* search for advocates. Did you forget?

For Those Who Remembered ...
If my training has had any real impact, you'll look forward to becoming a resource for those who are in transition and actively pursuing leads. You already know that the act of giving (or giving back) almost always cycles back to benefit you in some way or another, often unexpectedly.

Most ETP Network members who've landed hard-fought positions are more than willing to fill the role of a Group "B" Advocate ("cheerleader") to help others in transition connect the dots to a decision-maker.

8.6   Gather Business Intelligence

In addition to growing and maintaining your network, perhaps the most critical task is to gather business intelligence about your industry wherever and when-ever possible.

As you get to know the staff in terms of corporate and social hierarchies, keep your eyes and ears open. Industry news can be of enormous benefit, not only as you pursue future employment activities, but to others who may want you to act as an advocate.

8.7 Summary and Scoreboard

You've just read Chapter 8. In winning the race for 21st century jobs, you now know the following:

- You understand what really happens after all the hard work of getting an interview and landing the job.
- You understand why your networking activities must not be allowed to stop just because you're now back in "paycheck mode".

CORE CHAPTERS											
1	2	3	4	5	6	7	8	9	10	11	12
▲	▲	▲	▲	▲	▲	▲	▲				

You now have three options:

1. Ignore the rest of the book and move on to other things.
2. Slide back into the dead-end comfort of The Black Hole.
3. Move on to Chapter 9, *Putting It All Together and Troubleshooting*, to discover how all the pieces of this Career Management System fit together and how to troubleshoot the rough spots.

It's Your Decision.

Chapter 9
Putting It All Together and Troubleshooting

9.1 Just Fly the Plane!

As student pilots approach the end of their formal training, they take one last trip with their instructors before going up for that first nerve-wracking solo flight. Instructors report that some students become so obsessed with dials, gauges, and basic maneuvers that they forget one of the most important rules: **Sometimes you just have to sit back and fly the plane!** The preliminaries are over. You know the cockpit controls inside out. You know how the emergency procedures work.

At this point, you're ready for your ETP Network solo flight. You've fine-tuned the necessary connection and networking skills (Chapter 2), fully embraced the CEO of ME, Inc. mind- set (Chapter 3), tested your skill at crafting powerful, persuasive value propositions (Chapter 4) and mastered the 7-Step Job Search Methodology that will enable you to find the job best suited to your unique skills and abilities (Chapter 5).

You've also discovered the Hidden Job Market (Chapter 6), aced a few interviews (Chapter 7) and, landed a position as a result of your hard work (Chapter 8). That means that you are now in a unique position to continue your own career journey while remaining a valuable resource to others who are still *en route*.

Don't worry if you hit occasional turbulence such as neglecting to make a key follow-up call or perhaps misreading some core skills in a job description because those types of errors **will occur.** But by the time you've gone through a few complete cycles of the methodology, you will have acquired enough experience to claim that you "know where all the rough spots are." Having successfully navigated those rough spots, you now become someone who can lead others — and make no mistake, others **will** want to follow you to learn from your successes **and** your failures.

Right now, however, it's time for you to integrate all that you've learned into a single, seamless, and logical plan to manage your career as a business. To put it another way, it's now time for **you** to just fly the plane!

9.2 Putting It All Together — the Conceptual View

Let's take a look at what you've accomplished and decide what it all means. This is my high-level conceptual view:

What Have You Done?
You've acquired a whole new perspective on carrying out a job search. It's systematic, focused and demanding. If you've gotten this far, you have eliminated the GIGO

Principle (Garbage In, Garbage Out) from your modus operandi **forever.**

- You've assumed the position of a Chief Executive Officer. No more GIGO.

Where Have You Been?

You're now working from a position of personal power, the power you conferred upon yourself by adopting the CEO of ME, Inc. mental model as the key to managing your career. You've visited with HR managers at different companies, explored the Hidden Job Market, made numerous contacts at various networking events, attended membership conference calls and job search webinars, and probably even nailed a few interviews.

- You've been all over the job market landscape.

What Does It Mean?

If you've been diligent about developing your connecting and networking skills, managing your career as the CEO of a business, mastering the value proposition, and following the 7-Step Job Search Methodology, **you have successfully cut yourself loose from The Black Hole.** *You are now a fully vested CEO of your own business and an ETP Network member of the highest order. Why? Because now you know there's a system that really works and* **you** *know the ropes!*

- You are a believer.

Where Do I Stand in the Race for 21st Century Jobs?

Now that you're on the other side of those ropes, the career management landscape probably looks quite different. Now you're an accomplished networker, a savvy CEO of ME, Inc., an architect of high-impact value propositions, and a master of the 7-Step Job Search Methodology. You know the Hidden Job Market and can perform brilliantly for any interview. You are now a **career entrepreneur** *and will never think of yourself as a "job seeker" any more.* **You are at the head of the pack. The challenge now is to stay there!**

9.3 Putting It All Together — the Practical View

To really fly this methodology solo, you must be able to integrate the principles, procedures, and skills identified in the four "core chapters" found earlier in this book (i.e., Chapter 2, Networking; Chapter 3, CEO of ME, Inc. mind-set; Chapter 4, ETP Network Value Proposition; and Chapter 5, The 7-Step Job Search Methodology) into one smooth and seamless **megaskill** to the point that you don't need to think about them in order to execute them; just like the new pilot, you'll simply sit back and "fly the plane", allowing the skill components to mesh perfectly and perform flawlessly, all **on demand.**

Here are just a few practical examples of this integration:

- Master the art of small talk, connect with others as frequently as possible, develop relationships from those connections that seem interesting, and nurture the relationships so they can be added to your ever-expanding "warm trusted network". Never allow yourself to forget the importance of trust and reciprocity. *Your ability to connect and bond with others will bear fruit when it's time to contact advocates in Step # 5 of the 7-Step Job Search Methodology.*

- Discipline your mind to adopt a positive mental attitude and a degree of mental toughness that will see you through any of the job search or career management obstacles you may face. Become relentless in the pursuit of your goals. *When connecting with advocates or during an interview, let your upbeat business attitude and CEO-style strengths shine through. Make them work for you!*

- Think and act like a CEO. Exude confidence. Learn the traits of some highly effective CEOs and do your best to emulate them. Believe that you are truly the CEO of your career. Take responsibility for all of your actions and decisions. Start segmenting your job search tasks according to their "corporate function", i.e., R & D for networking, Sales & Marketing for interviews, etc... *Once you begin to think and act like a business owner, you effectively put your career management enterprise on a well-defined trajectory for success.*

- Become a PhD in job descriptions. You know what I mean ... they're often painfully dull, true, but they're the key to getting the job. *The more familiar you are with each position you intend to pursue, 1) the more solid your value proposition (see next point and 2) the more comfortable your interview will be.*

- Master the ETP Network Value Proposition (job description + targeted resume + targeted cover letter). This trio of documents is your one best chance for making a solid, compelling case that will attract decision-makers to you. *You learned how to develop the ETP Network Value Proposition in Chapter 4; but you applied it in Chapter 5,*

The Methodology: The 7-Step Job Search Methodology (Steps 4 & 5).

- Invest the time necessary to develop your personal brand. The ETP Network Value Proposition carries even more impact when targeted resume writers take the time to embed a unique tone, message, perspective, or theme that distinguishes him or her from the crowd. *A powerful personal brand is an invaluable asset throughout the 7-Step Job Search Methodology as well as excursions into the Hidden Job Market. Just be sure that you brand yourself; don't let others brand you.*

- Use social networking sites such as *LinkedIn, Twitter,* and *Facebook* to get your name and brand circulating. *The "buzz" you generate in the social mediasphere will be exceptionally helpful when it comes time to connect with Group "A" or Group "B" Advocates in the 7-Step Job Search Methodology as well as the Hidden Job Market ... why? Being able to clearly identify yourself as a thought leader in a particular space brings you instant and verifiable credibility.*

- Above all, leverage the power of social networking sites to make new connections. *The ability to forge online connections through these sites fuels the expansion of your network. Even better, social networking sites are open around the clock 365 days a year. Please bear in mind that social networking sites are all about networking (R & D), not selling (Sales & Marketing).*

- When it comes time for an interview, leverage the power of your ETP Network Value Proposition in which you've made your case for the position.

The qualification bullets on the right side of a powerfully optimized T-Letter will become your "talking points" (at the appropriate time, of course) during the interview.

There are many more examples that will surface throughout the rest of the book.

9.4 Troubleshooting

Now it's time to shift gears and **reverse** the thought process a bit (for learning purposes only). Now it's time to take the job search mosaic apart and examine 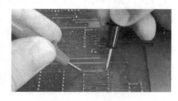 some of its rougher edges. We'll do this to deepen your understanding of the entire job search system and we'll focus on those areas in the job search methodology that can be especially troublesome.

It's time to do some troubleshooting.

I mentioned this earlier but it bears repeating. Just because you're "flying the plane", don't think for a minute that you'll be free from occasional turbulence. *You will make mistakes!*

But everyone makes mistakes. Even CEOs make mistakes because they're all human. So when you slip up and commit a Grade 'A' Blunder, the easiest way to regain control — and avoid further occurrences — is to find out what caused the error in the first place. I'd like you to consider the following information as a kind of *troubleshooting guide,* something to read and absorb *before* you embark on your next flight.

These are the "hot spots" that trip up more members than any others:

A. Failure To Adequately Understand The Job Description

This is probably *the* most egregious of all ETP Network job search errors. Think of it as a curse, the plague, or the gateway to hell — it doesn't matter what kind of mental association you use — just make sure you prevent it from happening.

You may think I'm being a little too melodramatic here. I don't think so. Here's why:

Failure to fully understand something as fundamental as a job description can throw your entire search off-course. If you fail to make an accurate match-up of the position's core skills with your own core skills, you will spend the a great deal of time preparing a targeted resume that isn't even close to the target — *all for nothing.*

Let's get specific. In almost every valid job description, you'll read about the company, the responsibilities, day to day work, etc... and then, usually at the bottom of the job description, you'll see a section for "core skills." *These* are the items around which you must build your case, your *value proposition.*

B. Unwillingness to Perform Due Diligence on Job Descriptions

There are individuals who absolutely hate to review job descriptions (7-Step Job Search Methodology, Step # 3). They'd prefer to outsource the work to an agency, a friend, or a neighbor's Siberian Husky if they thought they could get away with it.

But as business owners, we often must do things we don't like to do. It's a case of toughing it out. You didn't really think being a business owner was going to be a walk in the park, did you?

C. Writing Poorly Targeted Resumes

Do you have insomnia? Some people read dull books to help them fall asleep. Some count sheet. Me? I think about all the resumes that cross my desk every day claiming to be targeted resumes but which are light years away from the target. I worry about the authors of those resumes because they are evidently clueless concerning the whole point of a targeted resume.

Most of the offending documents are totally out of synch with the job description; in some, the author felt compelled to spew out every irrelevant factoid of her past, broadcasting her ignorance of even the most basic components of a targeted resume.

When you are in a full throttle job search, it's vital that you provide the client (decision-maker) with exactly what he or she is looking for, not just what you wish it **could** be.

Another key reason for crafting an expertly targeted resume is that today, people choose new talent via consensus hiring; in other words, **a team makes the decision.** And in case you didn't know it, **that team is looking to cut you from the herd.** The targeted resume gives them a powerful reason **not** to do that.

D. <u>Resumes with the Beauty of Picasso, but the Relevance of a Thumb Tack</u>

While I'm on the "relevance" bandwagon, let me highlight another common resume error. Some people are fascinated with appearance, layout, and things that look good on paper. They're convinced that if their resume *looks* spectacular, the document's *aura* alone will simply disarm unsuspecting decision-makers, causing them to go into an absolute swoon over you.

PSSST! Listen carefully ...

The only thing decision-makers are interested in is seeing **how you can add value** *to their company. That's it.* **Value.** *Not pretty documents. And the only way they can determine value is in your choice of words and whether or not you've made a bulletproof case that positions you as* **the one truly qualified candidate for the job.**

E. <u>The Only Way to Evaluate a Targeted Resume</u>

When seeking guidance in evaluating the quality of a targeted resume, remember that it can only be judged with reference to the position for which it was written.

Dave:

"Rod, I just re-worked my resume and I'm getting ready to submit it to one of my targeted positions. I'd like to have you take a look at it and give me some feedback."

mentor:

"Hey, Dave... that's terrific. It looks like a very professional piece of work."

Dave:

"Thanks Rod, but what I really need you to do is to evaluate how well I've built my case. I need you to focus on the writing, not the layout."

mentor:

"Gee, Dave... I'd love to help, but aren't we missing something here? How can I evaluate anything? I can only judge your words based on the specific job description to which you're responding. How can I judge whether this resume is good or bad if I don't even know what the goal is?"

"Show me the job description you're responding to, THEN I'll give you the feedback!!"

F. Resumes With Only Scattered Relevance in the Past 3 – 5 Years

One young woman had acquired the requisite core skills over the last 3 to 5 years, she just didn't acquire them all at the same company. In fact, she'd had three different positions in the last eighteen months. As such, here's the question she must be willing to ask a decision-maker:

"Given that I have all the skills you're looking for but at various companies, is that going to be a problem for me?

If so, perhaps I should consider another position; if not, what would you suggest as my next step?"

The beauty of this question is that she will get an answer either way. She'll be encouraged to pursue the position or she'll be advised that she's not a good fit. If it's the latter, she'll take the hint, say thank you, and confidently move on to the next opportunity. As a business owner, a CEO, she will not sink into deep despair if the answer is no; she will simply move on.

G. Failure to Follow Up

Along with Failure to Adequately Understand the Job Description (Section A, above) **this is a "Magnitude One" ETP Network Job Search Error.** It pains me to say this, but I've seen what looked like sure-fire landings vaporize because the candidate failed to do the appropriate follow-up work.

Since the beginning of this book, I have stressed the importance of follow-up. I don't care what method you use, a notebook, a spreadsheet, 3 by 5 cards, etc... *you absolutely MUST log and track your follow-up calls.* You may not want to, but recognizing that it's part of a CEO mentality to track critical information, you'll want to adjust your routine so that this becomes a habit.

H. Fear of Phoning and/or Messing Up The Phone Call

It's well known in the career management space that many networkers and job seekers are afraid to pick up the phone and call potential decision-makers. They believe their nervousness will show up in the quality of their voice. Or maybe they're afraid of stumbling over their own words during the conversation.

But let's think about this for a minute. Do you really mean to tell me that you don't **want** to call someone? Someone who could be the answer to your job search problems? Someone who could pave the way for an interview? Why not? If you're not willing to call someone who might be able to help you, then you absolutely need to get some personal coaching for your *phone-o-phobia*. If you can't get this corrected, a key channel of communications is cut off for you — and in the thick of a job search, that's a clear invitation for failure.

This phone fear has me so bewildered and concerned that I lose sleep over it, especially when I imagine one of our members freezing in his tracks at the mere thought of dialing a telephone number.

Because the problem affects a disturbingly large proportion of networkers, the ETP Network Leadership Team and I will be developing a webinar to help those who need to overcome their fear of phoning. Expect to see lots of simulations, role-playing, and phone-oriented group dynamics. And when you finish up, the telephone will be your greatest asset.

I. You Did What? As A Business Owner?

My wife once told me that if we were ever out in public and I noticed her slip showing, I should tell her immediately — which I do even to this day. In a similar way, I like to challenge ETP Network members when their CEO-style thinking shows signs of slippage. I never do it to ridicule or demean, I do it to foster self-discipline. Here's an example from my vast library of case studies:

Allyson (who just happens to be in "full gripe mode"):

"Rod, I don't have time to review 41 job descriptions. It's just too much. And it's gonna wreck my plans for the weekend, too."

Rod:

"Allyson, let me ask you a question. **As a business owner,** would you **ever ignore** 41 responses to an RFP that cross your desk? Especially knowing that one of them may be a **great client** for helping your business thrive and grow?"

Allyson:

"No, of course not."

Rod:

"Thank you, Allyson... have a wonderful weekend."

J. Selling Yourself Short

You don't have to be Sigmund Freud to know that people with low self-esteem frequently demean themselves in their interactions with others. Unfortunately, this is something that frequently requires professional counseling.

I don't perform psychoanalysis here in the ETP Network; I prefer that people who have self-esteem issues find solutions by working with their own community of behavioral health care professionals, particularly since there is no longer any stigma attached to seeking psychiatric treatment. This is important because job search success relies heavily on your ability to project confident, positive and assertive behaviors. The quicker the treatment for poor self-esteem, the sooner the positive results will become reflected in your job search.

K. Being Self-Absorbed

Self-absorbed people are easy to spot since they tend to drag their own lighting and makeup crews along with them — or so it seems.

If this describes you, you may very well be a Self-Absorbed Person (SAP). And you have the right to **remain** self-absorbed if that is your choice. Just make sure you understand the consequences: Your behavior is witnessed every day by an endlessly changing audience who for the most part are not **nearly** as fond of you as you are of yourself. Networking is about reciprocity, about helping others achieve their goals so they will help you achieve yours. **But before someone will want you in their network, they need to like you first.** If you appear to be a SAP, endlessly enraptured by yourself, I'd say you have a problem.

L. Whining About Networking

One of the truly odd things about networking groups is that they often attract individuals who don't like networking. That's right: They've just joined a networking organization but they don't like to network.

Well I'm proud to say that you don't **have** to love networking to join the ETP Network. But at the least, you must be receptive to learning new techniques to build connections and relationships.

Whenever I hear "I don't like networking..."I automatically think of an article I read not long ago that made this appalling statement:

> "At any given time, some 80% of all available jobs aren't posted in the classified ads or on the Internet job boards. So who gets those positions? D The 60% of people who say they landed their last job through networking!"

You may not **like** to network, but in today's employment market, you've **got** to network. Why? You are in a race for 21st century jobs. If that doesn't convince you, maybe this will — ask yourself the following question:

> "Do I prefer to stay unemployed or do I prefer to knuckle under and become part of the 60% who actively engage in networking and go on to find jobs?"

M. Failure to Maintain a Group "A" / Group "B" Advocate Worksheet

Think of the Advocate Worksheet as a compass that will guide you through the maze of contacts, connections, and decision-makers on the way to getting an interview. The goal is follow-up. If you fail to maintain this document, you are admitting that follow-up isn't important. Very few of us can recall the scheduling intricacies involved in setting up overlapping appointments with advocates for different positions. So keep track. Or, to put it another way **yet again,** *follow up or fail!*

N. "I Don't Like ..."

Hey! I don't like taking out the garbage, but I do it because it has to be done. I don't like filing my taxes every year but I do it because it has to be done. Please remember: You are a **business owner.** It doesn't matter if something you must do to support the business of ME, Inc. happens to be something you don't like. Get over it and just do it.

So are you a CEO or not? If that's a "yes", then remind yourself of this: Every day CEOs spend a great deal of time doing things they'd prefer not to; but they do them to benefit the company's bottom line.

O. Sidestepping "The Direct Approach"

Read the little conversation I had recently with Jorge and the two scenarios following it and tell me that avoiding the direct approach is **ever** better than using it:

Jorge:
"Rod, I'm concerned about having a gap in my experience within the last 8 months. Am I going to catch flak for that?"

Rod:
"You shouldn't. But let me show you both sides of the coin and you can draw your own conclusions."

Scenario # 1:
The interviewer asks you about those 8 months. You answer:

"Well, I went to Puerto Rico, worked on my tan, hung out with my friends, had a real good time."

The interviewer now **knows** that you're not serious about work and that the 8 months **is** a relevant factor in choosing you.

<u>Scenario # 2:</u>

The interviewer asks you about those 8 months. You answer:

"The economy has been pretty bad, so I've kept busy with training, networking, and building up my skill set. But I noticed that you're looking for someone with skills A, B, C, & D. You should know that at the last company I worked, I did A, B, C, & D and saved the company $ 9 million dollars. In light of that, will these 8 months without employment matter? I certainly will not have forgotten the skills I used at that company."

If you were the interviewer, would you have a problem giving serious consideration to this candidate (who used the "direct approach")?

9.5   The Phone Call

Ah, the phone call! This is where the rubber meets the road. Many professionals admit that placing phone calls, particularly to unfamiliar parties, is like trying to carry a 10-ton elephant up the north face of Mt. Everest in a raging snowstorm. What makes calling a network contact so difficult is that you don't want to sound like a  solicitor begging for a sale. The key is the philosophy behind your call. If you fall into immediate sales mode and tell the contact what you want, you'll fail. Why? Because it's all about **you.** You are not thinking in "reciprocity mode". Until you **can** think that way, your calls won't be productive.

The philosophy behind every call is simply to reconnect and exchange information. It's a networking call, not a sales call. If you feel your heart racing and the phone seems heavy, you are making the wrong call. *STOP!* Make the call but remember the goal is to simply reconnect and exchange information.

Phone Call Scenario #1: The Wrong Way

[Background: I am calling a friend who I worked with for five years but have not spoken to in six. Recently, I found his contact information.]

> **Rod:**
> *"Hi Bill, this is Rod Colón. We worked together at Mango Tango company several years ago. How are you?"*
>
> **Bill:**
> *"Rod — Wow, long time no hear. How are you and the family?"*
>
> **Rod:**
> *"Bill the family is good but I'm not doing so well. I'm looking for work and need your help."*
>
> **Bill:**
> *"Sorry to hear that but my company is not hiring. Why don't you send me your resume and I will see what I can do."*

Observations
- This is a waste of a potentially great opportunity.
- How would you feel if someone who you have not

spoken to in 6 years only called you for a job?

- You have no idea what they are doing these days, either personally or professionally.
- You have no reconnection point as a basis for follow up.
- It's a fairly safe bet that your resume will be put aside and limited action will be taken by your friend
- Bill (in this case) probably feels a bit "used."

Phone Call Scenario #2: The Better Way

[Background: I am calling a friend who I worked with for five years but have not spoken to in six. Recently, I found his contact information.]

Rod:
"Hi Bill, this is Rod Colón. We worked together at Mango Tango company several years ago. How are you?"

Bill:
"Rod – wow, long time no hear. How are you and the family?"

Rod:
"The family is great and I am doing well. Is this a good time to talk?"

Bill:
"Sure, what is going on?"

Rod:
"I have realized over the years that it is critical to network and keep connected. I wanted to make sure you had my contact information and see how things are going for you."

Bill:

"Sounds like a plan." (90% of the time your network associate will agree that networking and staying connected is critical)

Rod:

"I am networking with 100s of professionals and wanted to make sure you are tapped into my network. Bill how are you doing?"

(This is the critical question to the call – and super important that you LISTEN – 50% will answer positively and 50% will answer negatively)

Bill:
[Negative Response]

Rod:

(Listen intently) "Bill, I am sorry to hear about your situation. Through my network, we have access to many openings. Why don't you e-mail me your resume and I will do what I can to connect you to the right people."

— OR —

Bill:
[Positive Response]

Rod:

"Bill that's great! I'm glad things are going well for you. What are you so excited about?" (Listen intently and record as much of the information as possible and use it for future conversations)

9.6 Summary and Scoreboard

You've just read Chapter 9. In winning the race for 21st century jobs, you now know the following:

- You've learned how to see the "mosaic" of everything put together.
- You've examined some of the common errors made by new CEOs of ME, Inc. and how to troubleshoot them.

CORE CHAPTERS											
1	2	3	4	5	6	7	8	9	10	11	12
▲	▲	▲	▲	▲	▲	▲	▲	▲			

You now have three options:

A. Ignore the rest of the book and move on to other things.
B. Slide back into the dead-end comfort of The Black Hole.
C. Move on to Chapter 10, *Social Networking: Be A Part Of It*, to learn everything you'll need to know about the phenomenal power of social networking and its role in the 7-Step Job Search Methodology.

It's Your Decision.

Chapter 10
Social Networking: Be a Part of It!

10. 1   Social Networking in the Crosshairs

On December 20, 2008, in Denver, Colorado, a Continental 737 veered off the runway during takeoff and was suddenly engulfed in flames, forcing all 107 passengers and five crew members out of the aircraft in a fiery blaze of chaos and terror.

In the harrowing aftermath of the accident, passenger Mike Wilson sent a live "tweet" from his mobile phone to his *Twitter* account:

*"Holy f****** s***! I was just in a plane crash!" was his initial "tweet."*

While family members were relieved, news and media personalities remained puzzled: "How could anyone fleeing a burning aircraft have the presence of mind to "tweet" about the disaster?" they asked.

Mike knew the power of online social networking web sites and that they provided a means for sharing real time information. He also knew that one "tweet" informed hundreds of followers at once as opposed to making hundreds of individual cell phone calls.

Today, stories like this bubble up with increasing frequency all over the world because they expose the stark and often graphic impact made by social networking web sites like **LinkedIn, Twitter,** and **Facebook** on our daily lives.

But I want to discuss social networking far from the perspective of spectacular news stories or banner headlines. My goal is to inform readers about the power of social networking so they can add some real-time "high octane power" to an already well-tuned networking machine.

If you want to turbocharge your job search, you'll need to make social networking part of your master connection strategy. Of course you can reject the whole idea too. But with so many people competing for so few jobs, you have to ask yourself one question: "Do I really want to ignore a powerful new technology that's practically custom-made for making connections and building relationships?" In my view, your competitors have already answered that question with a powerful "No!" So I'm afraid that leaves you very little choice.

10. 2   What is Social Networking?

Social networking is the use of web-based applications to connectwith people who can help you reach your career and business goals while you help them reach  theirs.   There are many social networking web sites. Generally, they are applications designed to help you build a professional network that has almost unlimited potential for connecting people around the world.

From an ETP Network perspective, here are the most

important things you should know about social networking web sites:

- With the exception of *LinkedIn*, social networking sites don't directly factor into the 7-Step Job Search Methodology, but they **can and do** facilitate connecting and networking. For this reason alone, they receive special mention in this book.

- If you learned anything about networking in the previous chapters, you know that connecting with others is **critical** to your job search and to your business success as the CEO of ME, Inc. Need proof? Just try to get a job or sell products and services without connections!

- Many people resist the attraction of *Facebook, Twitter,* and *LinkedIn,* yet one of the best strategies available is to use them all and go for maximum exposure. Just watch out for **pitfalls** because there are several (see Section 10. 9).

- Social networking is what you make of it. Invest a lot of time or invest no time. It's entirely up to you.

- Social networking is **not** about selling; it's about **networking.** Your goal needs to be the formation of relationships.

- One of the most important reasons why the ETP Network suggests you commit to social networking is that it can help you find advocates for your job search. The exposure you can achieve on social networking sites practically guarantees it.

10. 3   Sounds Like a Lot of Extra Work ... Why Bother?

I'll tell you why you should bother, but first let's answer this question: **Why do people go online in the first place?**

The answer is simple: According to *eMarketer*, about 70% of U.S. households were on the Internet in 2008. What were they doing?

- Researching
- Sharing
- Shopping
- Communicating

If your next question is "Do I really have time to do all this online networking?", the answer will be no surprise: **If you want to win the race for 21st century jobs then yes, you must make the time!**

The time investment is reasonable: Writing occasional blog posts or replying to questions on *LinkedIn* or *Twitter* doesn't take very long. But the return on that investment is significant because your dialogue can be picked up by thousands or maybe even millions of Internet users simultaneously. Try accomplishing that through snail mail, the cell phone, or "texting!"

Here's another angle to consider: **Recruiters and decision-makers are using LinkedIn and other social networking sites more frequently to gather information about job applicants.** If you have any desire to shape their opinion of you, why wouldn't you get actively involved? At the very least, you should be on *LinkedIn* to build contacts, obtain introductions, ask questions, and support others. It doesn't take long for a recruiter to spot something special about you, something that's part of your personal brand — but to benefit from the process you must be actively engaged in it.

10. 4 If You Choose to Do It, Observe the Protocols

While there are very few hard and fast rules on social networking sites, there are guidelines and protocols you should follow to ensure a positive experience and avoid problems, conflicts, and confrontations:

- If you're going to participate in social networking, do it properly: Participate frequently, respond to questions, and portray your brand in a positive way.

- **Don't sell:** People want to know about you as a person **first** and that takes some time.

- The best strategy: Spend time listening and watching to get a "feel" for the dialog; then, gradually start participating.

- Always try to determine how you can **add value** to the comment stream.

- It's not about making impressions, **it's about making friends!** Friends will share the truth with you.

- Always begin by seeking advice or asking some questions.

10. 5   Standing Out in the Crowd

Belonging to a social networking web site involves a bit of tightrope-walking. You'll want to establish your presence among the members of the community and proceed carefully. Make sure you understand the community's guidelines. Once you understand the ground rules, you can ease into a comfortable rhythm of participation.

The other side of the tightrope is that sooner or later you'll want to differentiate yourself from others and to get your personal brand circulating through your profiles, communications, questions, answers, and so on.

To help you accomplish this differentiation, here are a few guidelines:

1. **Brand yourself** − Be sure of who you are, what you do, and what you know. Make sure you're presenting the "face" you want these online strangers to see. Make everything you say or do a vehicle for transmitting your "brand image" to this new online audience. (See the section on personal branding below and also in Chapter 12, *Break Away From the Pack*).

2. **Ask questions** − On sites such as *LinkedIn*, *Twitter*, and *Facebook*, the ability to pose questions to a seemingly endless chain of contacts is a powerful connection device. Why? If you ask excellent questions that provoke meaningful discussions, this distinguishes you as a "thought catalyst", a clear benefit for your personal brand.

3. **Answer questions** – The ability to step up and answer a question on a site like *LinkedIn* helps brand you as a *thought leader* or even an *expert* regarding the content of the question. This is especially true if your answer is well worded and shows a sincere desire to resolve a problem or issue.

Personal Branding

Your brand is your personal identity. It's what people remember about you when they can't see you. What's included in your brand? For starters, there's depth of knowledge, range of skills, willingness to make contribu-  tions, effective communication style, engaging personality, and physical appearance. You can also positively brand yourself by focusing on quality, adding value, being punctual and providing quick turnaround time.

The highly visible nature of social networking makes it more important than ever to be scrupulous about your "reputation management." Why? Anything connected to your name on the Internet is viewed as a reflection of your character and integrity.

To establish your personal brand and make it stick, you need to be both visible and memorable. Your words must pack a punch. Here are some strategies:

- Emphasize benefits, not features
- Be clear and concise
- Be unique
- Show your personality
- Be consistent and persistent

To see how your name is perceived on the Internet, a good practice is to "*Google* yourself." *Google* your name and see what comes up. If it's all favorable, then everything is OK. If it isn't, then you may need to clean up some of your "digital dirt." There are specific ways to do this, and one of the best starting points is simply to "*Google*" the term "digital dirt." You'll find links to articles that explain what the term means, examples, and most importantly, how to get rid of it.

10. 6   The Big Three for ETP

In the ETP Network, we place the greatest emphasis on *LinkedIn* because it is widely regarded as the most appropriate social networking site for developing business and professional connections. *Facebook* and *Twitter* are geared more for the truly social side of connections, however they have great value for learning about other people and exploring common interests.

LINKEDIN

Introduction

LinkedIn is a social network made up almost entirely of business professionals. It is not really about social interactions; rather, it's designed for networking between people within the same industry and across industries. As social networking sites go, it's not very glamorous but for business purposes, it's got the best practical advantage since it allows anyone to build a network.

LinkedIn's Features and Advantages:
You can:

- Maintain online resumes and link with friends, colleagues, and business contacts
- Find experts that can help you with career or job search problems
- Connect directly with any *LinkedIn* account holder without the need for an introduction (provided you have a premium membership).

To really appreciate the power and value of *LinkedIn*, you first need to appreciate the concept of *"six degrees of separation."* This principle states that if we are each one step away from every person 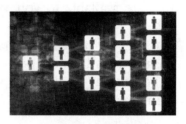 we know, then we are two steps away from every person **they** know. That means everyone on Earth is, at most, only six degrees away from every other person.

A simplified illustration of six degrees of separation might go like this:

You probably know Clint Eastwood!

Well, not directly. But you know David Jones (someone you know directly, called a "LinkedIn Level 1 connection"); David knows Melissa Stone (and therefore has access to her network); Melissa knows Julie Smith, a media consultant in Los Angeles; Melissa knows Mike Simpson, a talent agent for many Hollywood stars, and Mike, of course, knows Clint Eastwood. If you trace the path of these connections, you'll see a pattern in which you are never more than "six links" away from someone you'd like to reach.

LinkedIn's Popularity Trap

Some *LinkedIn* users get trapped into thinking that the name of the game is to gather as many Level 1 connections as possible. They put themselves in an undeclared popularity contest, proclaiming that they have, for example, "8,477 Level 1 connections." While their Level 1 numbers are certainly impressive, they regrettably miss both the point and the power of *LinkedIn*.

The **real** power of *LinkedIn* lies in the linkages that feed into your Level 1 connections, that is, the Level 2s and 3s that are available to you **via** your Level 1s. It is here in the "2/3 Zone" that the magnitude of your network becomes far more quantifiable; for example, 297 Level 1 connections balloon out to possibly tens of thousands of contacts at Level 2, and perhaps hundreds of thousands (or more) at Level 3.

This is an important point because research shows that the **vast majority of LinkedIn users who are actively engaged in a job search find their next job through their Level 2 and Level 3 connections, not their Level 1 connections.**

LinkedIn's Biggest Benefits

There have been many books written about *LinkedIn*, most notably I'm On *LinkedIn* – Now What? by ETP Network member Jason Alba. Jason uses a no-holds barred style of writing to explore all the good points about *LinkedIn* and to expose its weaknesses, too. It's a well-written and balanced analysis of the application by a man who truly understands how online applications are best engineered to serve the needs of users.

The biggest benefits of *LinkedIn* are as follows:
  • Use connections to explore a treasure chest of

hidden opportunities (see Chapter 6, *The Hidden Job Market*).

- Get your name and brand circulating right from your computer.
- Build your database of connections to strengthen your network.
- Quickly attain expert status.
- Get instant feedback.
- Network 24 x 7 x 365. Unlike traditional face-to-face networking, the Internet never sleeps.
  LinkedIn Groups give you access to individuals who are passionate about what *you're* passionate about.
- This makes for easier, faster connections.

FACEBOOK

Facebook is a social networking web site that is owned and operated by Facebook, Inc. You can join networks organized by location, workplace, school, and region to connect and interact with other members. *Facebook* allows users to add friends to their network, exchange messages, and post updates about current activities and projects.

One of *Facebook's* biggest benefits is the ability to establish connections and develop relationships at a comfortable pace based on the truly personal side of  human relationships. Having said that, many users also discover new business relationships within their circle of *Facebook* friends and go on to establish themselves as Level 1 connections on *LinkedIn*.

As with anything else in life, there are some risks and pitfalls associated with regular *Facebook* use, especially with regard to the issue of others posting content about you that may be unflattering, unkind, or even untrue. While that may not bother you personally, don't forget that *Facebook* is used by all sorts of people including HR managers and decision-makers who might just have the inclination to see if you are actively engaged in social networking and, if so, what you're saying, how you're saying it, and yes — it's true— what others are saying about you. They can develop impressions of you without ever having met you!

TWITTER

Twitter is often described as a "microblogging" site because you only get 140 characters to tell people *"what you're doing now"*. It's a great tool for tossing out questions to a large audience, getting quick answers, and staying connected to people who can help you in your career and job search efforts.

Twitter's job search value is centered on making connections. In addition, the bite-sized chunks of information help you stay focused and "on point" when you write.

10. 7 Blogs and Blogging

Many people ask "Should I be blogging?"

Blogging allows you to offer your thoughts, insights, and opinions to the online community; it gives them a "view" of who you are and how you think.

If you're new to blogging, here's a great tip: Start by *not* blogging at all, at least not right away. Instead, simply visit the blogs of others, especially those who share your interests. If you post meaningful comments on their blogs, you'll be setting the stage for reciprocal visits once you settle into a comfortable posting routine.

Again, as with *LinkedIn, Facebook, and Twitter*, don't sell. Instead, use your blog platform to create intrigue and build a following. Better yet, try to develop a community in which your blog posts become the spoke of a giant "wheel of common interest" and you'll have followers in no time. Ultimately, as you grow online relationships through blogging, you'll learn to gauge the right time for selling what you, the CEO of Me, Inc. has to offer.

10. 8   The Inbound Marketing Model

Social networking is built on the *inbound marketing model.* Inbound marketing refers to non-intrusive methods of reaching customers by providing something of value that gets noticed, discussed, and freely shared across a wide swath of the online population. It's built on the premise that attracting customers to you by providing something of value produces greater benefits than the traditional outbound marketing model which includes intruding on strangers with unsolicited e-mail, phone calls, faxes, etc. — often generating nothing but resentment.

With inbound marketing, you create compelling content, post it on your blogs, and attract the online community because you have something interesting to offer. Because the medium is based on permission, conversations occur because both parties agree to participate and want to be present.

---

10. 9   The Pitfalls of Social Networking Sites

I'm sure there's an entire laundry list of the pitfalls for social networking sites. I don't want to consume too much space with this, so I'll offer just a few. You can easily find more online.

The Personal Accountability Issue
Be careful of what you post online: The Internet saves all its input and there's no telling where something could re-surface at a most inopportune time. If that occurs while you're in job search mode, the results could be disastrous. Think twice before posting.

The Lack of Total Control Issue
Let's say you posed in a bikini last summer and the photograph, while flattering, was just a little bit provocative. Now let's say a friend posts that photo on *Facebook*. And now let's suppose that the individual you hope to have an interview with spots the same picture. It was nothing *you* did; but you cannot control what others do and some of their actions can unintentionally hurt you.

The Time Issue
You have to watch how you spend your time; online networking *can* become a major time sink, so it's up to you to manage that time. Set limits!

The Addiction Issue

At all costs, avoid the temptation to use social networking as your *only* networking venue; for the sake of your sanity and your job search, you still need a lot of "face time" with living, breathing human beings.

10. 10   The Lighter Side of Social Networking

Social Networking has a lighter side, too. Here are just a few anecdotes collected from various web sites that report on some of the more bizarre aspects of social networking today:

1. *Two students at Radford University in Virginia decided to do a little shoplifting in a clothing boutique. Not very smart. But far worse for them, they decided to post pictures of themselves modeling the fantastic outerwear on Facebook. The store owner/ Facebook member found the incriminating images and contacted local police.*

2. *A woman on Twitter was shocked to discover that her husband had just filed for divorce. Clearly, this wasn't what the originators of Twitter had in mind in terms of exchanging small bits of news, but hey! — it's a free country.*

3. *A young couple flew to the Bahamas for vacation. While there, they caught an iguana, killed it, and then cooked it. Unaware that the iguana is on the list of endangered species, the couple posted photos of their iguana meal on Facebook. Busted!*

10. 11 Summary and Scoreboard

You've just read Chapter 10. In winning the race for 21st century jobs, you now know the following:

- You've learned all about the value of joining social networking web sites.

- You've discovered how social networking can significantly increase the number of new connections.

	CORE CHAPTERS										
1	2	3	4	5	6	7	8	9	10	11	12
▲	▲	▲	▲	▲	▲	▲	▲	▲	▲		

You now have three options:

1. Ignore the rest of the book and move on to other things.
2. Slide back into the dead-end comfort of The Black Hole.
3. Move on to Chapter 11 to learn how the awesome power of attitude and behavior can have a phenomenal affect on your job search.

It's Your Decision.

Chapter 11

The Awesome Power of Attitude and Behavior

11.1 You're on Display — Constantly

A few weeks ago, two newly hired employees reported for work at a large electronics company in northern New Jersey. The company allowed them to bring just one carton of personal effects to their assigned desks.

Mario carried his belongings down the aisle separating the cubicles and stopped along the way to say hello and introduce himself. As the CEO of his own career, he knew that the machinery of networking never stops — not even when he walked into a new position. Those who smiled back to welcome him seemed genuinely impressed with his polite, positive, and upbeat behavior. He made a top-notch first impression.

In sharp contrast, Steve stormed down the same aisle, grumbling about how slow the elevator was, greeting no one, in fact even brushing a few people aside as he hurried to reach his office, finally slamming his box down on the desk with a loud groan. Over the cubicle walls, employees heard a stream of profanity as some of the larger books perched on top of the box fell to the floor.

There you have it! Instant first impressions. Two new employees, one company, and two radically different assessments by their co-workers about who is going to be easier to work with. ***Your attitude and behavior matter a great deal!***

It's important to understand that the lion's share of success in a successful job search is tied directly to an individual's attitude and resulting behavior. I have coached professionals in transition who were, for example, top-of-the-line computer programmers: brilliant, detail-oriented, meticulously organized, and 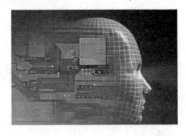 experienced beyond comprehension — only to discover that they tripped themselves up during an interview by doing something or saying something uncharacteristically foolish.

So in this chapter, we will deal with the heavy lifting of the job search that takes place ***entirely*** in your mind. There are no documents to write and no phone calls to make. You don't need to make connections or build relationships. Instead, you'll learn the business basics of attitude and behavior and, as the CEO of ME, Inc., you'll learn how to take control of them and leverage them for maximum personal advantage.

11.2 Take Charge of Your Attitude

Take charge of your attitude.
It's good advice, especially when you consider that no one else in the world can do it for you. But taking charge of

your attitude can be an enormous task, so let's understand what you're up against.

Although attitudes can make or break us, we **do** have the ability to change them. As with most challenges, it may not be immediately comfortable, but with a reasonable amount of effort you can learn to manage your attitudes and behaviors as easily as you manage your wardrobe. It all comes down to what you choose to display to the world from your "attitude menu."

As business owners, we need to keep a watchful eye on attitude and behavior because they have an enormous impact on friends, associates, and clients — not to mention our Personal Board of Directors. You can't expect to be a successful business owner if you have a chip on your shoulder, wear a perpetual frown, or allow jets of steam to shoot out of your ears just because you didn't get your way on an important conference call.

Negative Thinking vs. Negative Attitude
They're close — but not identical. Negative thinking is also called *negativity, being negative,* or just plain *pessimism.* People who think negatively often have deep, unresolved self-esteem issues. As a result, they put themselves down, are self-blaming, and have great difficulty with assertiveness.

Negative attitude (or in today's jargon, just *'attitude'*) carries the stigma of being disagreeable, unpleasant, unkind, pessimistic, deceptive, and so on. If you have negative attitudes about life or business, most of your challenges will come from people who've made the decision to ignore your toxic personality. Clearly, this will not help you get far in a job search!

In an outstanding article called "The Consequence of Attitude" published in 2005, Dr. Peter DeJager (pdaejager@technobility.com) identified numerous attitude problems that employees sometimes bring to the workplace. These include being:

Lazy/doing the minimum	Gossipy
Disrespectful	A clock watcher
Insubordinate	A prima donna
Negative	Defensive
Unhappy	Argumentative
Pessimistic	Deceitful
Unwilling to offer solutions	Abrasive
Surly	Rude
Disruptive	Confrontational
Sarcastic	Inflexible
Contentious	Unpleasant

If this list describes you either in whole or in part, you should expect an additional barrier to becoming an effective CEO of ME, Inc. Again, *most businesspeople will not tolerate negative attitudes. Instead, they'll simply detach themselves from any meaningful relationship with you.*

No One Values Negativity
Negative thinking, negative attitude, and negative behavior are all frowned upon —especially here in the ETP Network. *But that doesn't necessarily spell doom.*

Here's an anecdote from my attitude and behavior archives to illustrate my point:

> *A middle-aged man called me in late August, 2007 asking if he could retain my services as a career coach. He was in a huge slump and hurting financially. He had recently sustained a debilitating injury and faced a long period of physical therapy. He wanted to get more actively involved in making meaningful connections, networking, and effective job searching but felt that his intense shyness stood in his way. I had originally planned to offer him some basic coaching services but then thought better of it. It would have been an exercise in futility.*

> *"I'm sorry, Dan D I've decided not to coach you at this time", I told him. I could tell that my decision startled him. "Why?", came his response. "Because I would be unable to make any progress with someone who enters the partnership carrying such a negative attitude. We would spend a full month just trying to get your attitude fixed. We'd be wasting a lot of my time and your money trying to fix a problem that only you can control. I don't mean to hurt your feelings or offend you by telling you this, but right now it's your negative attitude that's the primary obstacle to progress and nothing else. Once you figure out how to adjust the inner man so you can visualize success and successful outcomes, then call me back and we'll discuss a program that will help you."*

> *I found out later that Dan, far from being put off by this response, actually found the candor quite refreshing. He gave it a great deal of thought and we stayed in touch. He started writing some articles about networking which I decided to publish on the ETP Network web site. His attitude started to shift. Even his telephone persona sounded much more upbeat.*

Today, he's a member of my leadership team, a strategic business partner, and a close personal friend.

You Are What You Think You Are

Henry Ford once said "Whether you think you can or think you can't, you're right."

I'm always amazed when individuals come to me with statements of defeat, hopelessness or frustration such as "Rod, I just can't write a good T-Letter ... it's hopeless!" or "Rod, I keep striking out during interviews."

Don't misunderstand: I'm not amazed that they confide in me. I'm amazed that they expect me to wave a magic wand and make the problem go away. So to keep the spotlight of responsibility properly focused on the only person who can solve the problem, I use a technique called **bounce back.** Here are three examples:

Jorge:
"Rod, I'm no good at writing resumes."

Rod:
"Jorge, you're right ... you're no good at writing resumes."

Melissa:
"Rod, I can't use the telephone to call advocates; I'm just too shy."

Rod:
"Melissa, you're right ... you can't use the telephone to call advocates; you're just too shy."

Stephan:
"Rod, I'm a failure."

Rod:
"Stephan, you're right ... you're a failure."

Is this harsh? I don't think so. I'm not slamming a door in anyone's face and they all know deep inside that I'm just trying to break down an obstacle that's preventing both of us from making progress.

But what I'm **really** trying to do with this technique is to get people to see that **they are whatever they truly believe they are.** It's like this: If you **think** that something really is a certain way, then guess what? **It really is!** Your thoughts and attitudes become "causation triggers" for the very condition you're complaining about! I'm confident that Henry Ford would agree with me.

The solution? Stop complaining! Start thinking positively even if it hurts. Just do it! No one has to stay mired in the muck of negativity. It's time to display a positive face for the world and enjoy all of the successes that are out there waiting for you ... **so go after them!**

Positive Attitudes Blend with the CEO of ME, Inc.
Anyone can **willfully** adopt the right attitude. No matter where you're from or how much innate talent you have, the right attitude can make a difference in your career. Try adopting these 10 attitudes of successful workers (from an article by Kate Lorenz, Editor, *CareerBuilder.com*):

1. *I am in charge of my destiny.*
   If you want something bad enough, you must "make it happen." Don't expect good fortune to fall out of

the sky and into your lap. There's a huge difference between wanting something and executing a well-planned strategy for obtaining it.

2. *Anything is possible.*
   Many of us blindly accept the notion that some things are just "impossible." As a result, we often make no attempt to reach for them. The reality is that people around the world achieve what they previously considered *impossible* by being relentless in their pursuit of it.

3. *No task is too small to do well.*
   Those who are serious about getting ahead in life assign importance to all tasks, regardless of their size. They realize that others are watching and evaluating their performance — even on the small stuff.

4. *Everyone is a potential key contact.*
   None of us ever know ahead of time who will become a key contact or perhaps an important business ally. That means it's essential to treat everyone with dignity and respect at all times.

5. *I was made to do this job ... and the one above me.*
   Enthusiasm is contagious. When you bring enthusiasm to the table, you get noticed ... and you never know when someone noticing could turn out to be a key decision-maker.

6. *It's not just what I know, but who I know.*
   It's unwise to entrust your personal success to your intellect alone, smart as you may be. In the 21st century jobscape, you must become a masterful connector and networker. It's more important now than ever before to understand the economic power contained within relationships.

7. ***What else can I do?***

We're all busy and we only get 24 hours in a day. But taking on extra work, volunteering, and offering time without getting paid for it is a sign of someone who is committed to success. This is the kind of energy and commitment that gets noticed — and rewarded!

8. ***Failure helps pave the way to success.***

It sounds odd, but failure is often the best thing that can happen to us. Why? It highlights weaknesses and imperfections, providing a perfect starting point for new growth.

9. ***I am my own biggest fan.***

When does exuding self-confidence cross the line into bragging? Most CEOs know how to display a healthy self-image without letting it get out of control. And it's important to understand this: Having a healthy self-image is part of what makes you attractive to the business community.

10. ***My opportunity monitor is never turned off.***

Opportunities are all around us all the time; it's just that many of us "tune them out" when we get extra busy or pressed for time. The opportunity monitor must be left in the "on" position so that the truly great ones don't slip by unnoticed.

11.3 Take Charge of Your Behavior

Attitudes drive behaviors. Thinking like the CEO of ME, Inc.— genuinely believing in every step you take—

will drive the corresponding business behaviors.
But you can't fake it. You can't *pretend* to embrace the
CEO paradigm. If you haven't genuinely embedded it in
your mind or if you don't actually believe it can work,
you may as well put this book on the shelf next to your
collection of *National Geographic* or perhaps use it as
a paperweight.

The Dark Side of Behavior

Psychologists have been
studying behavior ever
since it was first recog-
nized as a human trait.
Then sociologists stepped
in to differentiate "good
behavior" from bad. Let's

spend a few minutes examining the bad behavior ele-
ments that can sabotage business owners trying to successfully manage their own careers.

As with attitude, *behavior is always in the spotlight.* The only
real difference is that while attitude can often be hidden,
behavior cannot. Once bad behavior is on display, it can
remain etched in the minds of those around us for a long
time. **There is no "undo" button for bad behavior.**

Have you ever watched someone make an absolute fool
of himself in a meeting? Or perhaps you were exposed
to a particularly nasty verbal assault by a manager or col-
league? Now think: Did you immediately brush it off or
did the incident linger in your mind? The recollection
of these highly charged negative episodes can last a
long time, especially when **we** are the ones who've
been victimized.

Here are some of the really bad business behaviors that will put you back at *Square One* in your job or client search:

- Taking credit for the efforts of others
- Shifting blame for your own mistakes
- Checking e-mail or texting during a meeting
- Sending bad news through e-mail to avoid facing the recipient
- Talking down to others
- Crossing the line between being assertive and being aggressive
- Gaining a reputation for procrastination
- Gaining a reputation for being deceitful and/or dishonest
- Failing to listen intently
- Spreading rumors about colleagues
- Setting others up for failure
- Showing up late or leaving a meeting early with no explanation
- Belittling the efforts of colleagues
- Leaving snippy voice mail or e-mail messages
- Forwarding others' e-mail to make them look bad
- Making demeaning or derogatory remarks to someone
- Behaving as if you are entitled to things (entitlement mentality)
- Withholding information
- Failing to return phone calls or respond to e-mail
- Leaving a mess for others to clean up
- Consistently grabbing easy tasks while leaving difficult ones for others
- Shutting someone out of a network or team
- Paying little attention or showing little interest in the opinions of others
- Off-putting (*"That's not **my** problem ..."*)

Again, if you find yourself anywhere on that list, I caution you to clean up your act now before you become actively engaged in the ETP Network job search methodology. You **must** learn to have complete control of your behavior so that it never becomes a barrier to progress.

This Is Not the Occasional "Bad Day"

We all have "bad days." No one goes through life without them. But there's a huge difference between having a bad day and consistently being cranky, irritable, impatient, pompous, vengeful, devious, dishonest, mean, or surly. The operative word here is "consistently."

If any of the words in the preceding paragraph describe you, you may have a problem for which you should seek help. On the other hand, if you rarely exhibit these behaviors, some good coaching will enable you to handle the occasional rough spots in a more professional way. The benefits of this pre-emptive action are clear: It smoothes the path toward successful social interaction and to stronger relationships with members of your own warm, trusted network.

Please don't come to me or my leadership team for "behavior counseling" — we don't offer psychotherapy here because we're neither trained nor licensed to perform it. We can, however, offer advice and guidance (if asked) and in an organization such as the ETP Network with thousands of experienced professionals representing every possible industry, there will surely be someone with the appropriate credentials who can help you.

Finally, any good bookstore has a "self-help" section with many resources for attitude and behavior adjustments. It's also possible that a discussion with a behavioral specialist might help. But don't put it off. As the CEO of a business, you owe it to yourself and to those who depend on you to manage your personal issues as effectively as you manage your business affairs.

11.4 Confronting Fear, Anxiety and Depression

It's normal for individuals in transition to experience fear, worry, anxiety and depression. Since these feelings are the *natural* by-products of the stress brought on by unemployment, it could be argued that the *absence* of these emotions might indicate an even deeper problem.

The loneliness, hopelessness, and sadness of depression can make you afraid and anxious. In turn, this fear and anxiety can exhaust you and make you more depressed. It's a vicious cycle.

Unfortunately, there are no magic bullets to deal with these conditions, but within our network, there are countless doctors, counselors, behavior specialists, and other professionals who can be contacted for assistance.

Furthermore, there is no shame attached to seeking this kind of help. Many people actively seek counseling when the stress and pressure of our complex technological society bubble to the surface and become unmanageable.

The important thing is to tame the behavior monster and get it under control. As we often hear, *"perception is reality."* What people *perceive* you to be is what they really believe you are.

So the next time you have any of these reactions ...

- Jumping to conclusions ("I just *knew* they hated my speech ... ")
- Tunnel vision ("I didn't get the interview because my T-Letter was too vague...")
- Overgeneralization ("New Yorkers only like to hire other New Yorkers ...")
- Personalization ("I really, really messed things up this time ...")
- Mind reading ("I'll bet they're thinking that I'm just a no good ...")
- Emotional reasoning ("My boss is such an incredible jerk! ...")

... take a deep breath, calm down, and readjust your attitudes and behaviors. Remember, if you show someone your worst side, they're going to remember it. As the CEO of ME, Inc., the last thing you need is an attitude that offends or a behavior that alienates. *So "let's be careful out there!"*

11.5   Learn From Your Failures

If nothing succeeds like success, where does that put failure? Should we make a concerted effort to avoid failure at all cost? Of course. But it's totally unrealistic to think that we will be 100% successful in avoiding failure; human nature will eventually catch up with us and deliver a predictably swift dose of reality.

What *is* important is what we do with *"error aftershock."* Some individuals become so obsessed with their failures that they become unable to reframe their thinking to prevent the mistake from reoccurring.

But failure is instructive. We would never have learned anything in school if we hadn't failed from time to time. In fact, one of the great secrets of academia (which I only learned after I'd been out of school for quite some time) is that teachers actually *expected* us to fail occasionally. How can this be good?

Struggling to learn or accomplish something puts up a flag that says, "OK, I know "A" very well, but I'm having difficulty with "B", and I really don't get "C" at all. However I do know where to look for help or who can be a resource." As long as your failure "exit strategy" is aimed at healthy correction instead of pointless self-condemnation, failure can still be a positive learning experience.

When you fail at making connections, forming relationships, adopting the CEO of ME, Inc. mind-set, messing up your value proposition, or failing to fully vet a job description, treat the failure as an opportunity for correction. And most importantly, don't internalize the mistake. It's just a business error and businesses make errors every day of the year. Just learn how to recover from it and avoid it next time.

11.6   Make the Tough Decisions

The fact that you've come this far in the book and stayed with it means you have the tenacity to make the 7-Step Job Search Methodology work for you. This will greatly reduce the amount of time you spend in transition.

But you **will** make some very difficult decisions along the way. Since there's no magic wand you can wave to help you make these choices, please consider the following helpful guidelines:

- ALWAYS accept full responsibility for your decisions, regardless of outcome.

- Difficult decisions are good litmus tests for character and judgment; you may not make the best choice every time, but it's your overall "batting average" that matters most, not any single trip to the plate.

- No one ever said you had to make tough decisions in a vacuum; as a CEO, you will probably want to consult with your on-staff experts or network contacts for information and help in the decision-making process.

- Whatever you do, never give up responsibility for making a key decision. On the *Rod Colón Error Scale* (0 to 10, 10 being the worst), this is an easy 9. Making no decision at all (i.e., abandoning the decision-making process due to fear or timidity) is far worse than making the world's single most hideous decision about anything. Think about it.

11.7 The Field of Battle is Here

In following my Job Search Methodology, most of the real problems you'll encounter will not come from methodology errors or failing to ping someone regularly. The really tough battles will almost always be the ones you fight within your own mind: your thoughts, perceptions, fears, frustrations, and the demons of indecision.

You can become the most knowledgeable student of the 7-Step Job Search Methodology and **still** run into problems making it work if you fall prey to excessive fear, worry, anxiety or depression.

Here's what you can do about this:

> *Many psychologists believe that the mind can process only one thought at a time. When a new thought enters the mind, the previous thought is pushed aside; it's not actually lost because memory can retrieve it, but the two thoughts never occupy your consciousness simultaneously.*

> *It's similar to a demonstration you may have seen in high school physics where the teacher dropped a large object into a cylinder filled with water. The mass of the object displaced the water, pushing it upward.*

> *When the object was removed from the cylinder, the water returned to its original level.*

The lesson: No two objects can occupy the same place at the same time; the large object goes in, the water level goes up. Remove the large object and the water returns to its original level.

It's pretty much the same way with the human brain.

If you consciously make an effort to think positive thoughts when you're feeling down, these positive thoughts can and will displace the negative thoughts and you'll notice a gradual improvement in your state of mind. But you have to persevere.

I can't guarantee this will work for you, but I know it's worked very well for me and for others who've tried it. It's worth a shot, don't you think?

11.8   It's All in Your Mind

If you need to know where the most challenging part of the 21st century job search lies, it lies in your mind. All of the decisions, judgments, analysis, creativity, discipline, mental toughness, and positive mental attitude are all situated in those 9 – 10 inches between your ears. You need to become comfortable in exercising control over these capabilities in order to steer a successful course toward your next position, your next contract, or your next career.

We've already seen evidence in earlier parts of this book of just how important the exercise of mental control really is. In fact it's at the "core of the core" — that is to say, each of the four **core chapters** in this book (listed below) deals with topics that are heavily dependent on an individual's exercise of mental control.

1. Small Talk/Connections/Relationships/Networks/ Warm, Trusted Networks *(Chapter 2):*

   Your mind must be receptive to the challenges of meeting new people. If you're a natural extrovert, hey — no problem! But if you're introverted, shy, or excessively nervous when meeting others, this very first "baby step" toward solid networking can be exceedingly awkward.

2. Adopt a CEO mind-set in the way you run the business of managing your career *(Chapter 3):*

   It's fair to say that this component of my job search system is really "pure attitude driving pure behavior" and that an attitude of success will foster successful outcomes.

3. Master the art of creating an absolutely brilliant value proposition, one that no hiring manager could possibly ignore *(Chapter 4):*

   This requires healthy, high self-esteem, an eager and persistent drive to prove your worth to a decision-maker, and an understanding that these attitudes will create the desired outcomes.

4. Execute the 7-Step Job Search Methodology that will guide you from the discovery of an exciting opportunity all the way to snagging the interview *(Chapter 5):*

   The attitude: I will be mentally tough and remain focused on these specific tasks and subtasks. The behavior: Carry out tasks as prescribed; follow up, and continually prospect for new opportunities.

A Final Word About Attitude

To run a ME, Inc. business successfully, you have to be **excited** about the product you're offering (which is **you**). If you're not excited, how can you expect others to be? Why bother to sell, brand, and network if you're not excited about your own business? Become **excited** about yourself, your business, and your place in the race for 21st century jobs!

11.9 Summary and Scoreboard

You've just read Chapter 11. In winning the race for 21st century jobs, you now know the following:

- Attitude and behavior are critical components of a successful job search.
- Attitude and behavior are under the control of each individual.

	CORE CHAPTERS										
1	2	3	4	5	6	7	8	9	10	11	12
▲	▲	▲	▲	▲	▲	▲	▲	▲	▲	▲	

You now have three options:

1. Ignore the rest of the book and move on to other things.
2. Slide back into the dead-end comfort of The Black Hole.
3. Move on to Chapter 12 to learn about the things that you can do to establish yourself as a front-runner in the race for 21st century jobs.

It's Your Decision.

Chapter 12
Break Away From the Pack

12.1 Dare to Tap Your Full Potential

A few years ago, there was an automobile accident that got widespread media attention because of the heroic actions of a young mother in saving her 5-year-old daughter's life. In the aftermath of the accident, the child had become pinned under the wheel of a car and was probably moments from death when the woman summoned the strength to lift the rear bumper– just high enough to permit her son to pull his sister to safety!

We sometimes hear stories like this and think, "That's amazing! Could I have done the same thing under similar circumstances?"

I'm here to tell you that the answer is a resounding *"YES!"*

We can all perform at levels far greater than we ever believe possible. And that's part of the problem. Most of us never stop to think about the size and scope of our own potential. It's just not a hot item on today's "to do" list.

Since the final chapter of any book is a good place to offer challenges to readers, I'd like to toss a few out to you ... three, to be exact:

1. **First,** I challenge you to begin exploring the hidden reserves of physical strength and mental stamina you didn't know you had. *The objective:* Find out if you can do the supposedly impossible task. **Really push yourself and push hard!**

2. **Second,** assuming you were successful with the first challenge, I now challenge you to shift that vast untapped ability onto your daily radar screen. Make a genuine effort to see it, think it and feel it all of the time. As the CEO of ME, Inc., allow it to become the driving force behind your day-to-day business decisions. *The objective:* Make your *extended capabilities* the *standard* for everything you do.

3. **Third,** I challenge you to take the ETP Network for a "test drive." There is no cost or obligation. Put yourself through the paces for a month or two. Participate in our regularly scheduled programs and learn the unique 7-Step Job Search Methodology in a friendly, supportive environment that COO Carl Reid describes as a "safe harbor." Try to pick up the rhythm of the job search as I've outlined it in this book. *The objective:* See how much more you achieve — and how much better it feels — when **you put yourself in charge** of all your career management decisions.

Why the challenges?
Let's think again about the woman who lifted a car to save her child. Now let's relate that story to the title of this book — "Win the Race for 21st Century Jobs."

Do you really think you have a chance to **win** this **crucial race** — or even stay in it at all — if you **don't** push yourself? And I mean really, truly **push?** Will you be content doing what everyone else is doing in the same way they're doing it? Are you willing to settle for cookie-cutter mediocrity knowing that an unknown number of others may be putting 10, 100, or even 1,000 times more effort into their searches?

Back to the woman who lifted the car: She could have flagged down a passing motorist to help her, but she didn't. There was no time. There was just one Herculean obstacle separating her from her child's survival. She chose a bold, decisive, almost superhuman action to meet the challenge — and that split-second decision saved her daughter's life.

With that in mind, stay focused on one key idea as you read this chapter:

In the race for 21st century jobs you have competition — ***lots of it.*** *As the total number of competitors increases, the ability to distinguish yourself becomes more and more difficult yet more and more necessary.*

Make a decision to face that challenge head-on. Commit to the idea of expecting more of yourself and **break away from the pack!**

12.2 The Case for Personal Branding

To win the race for 21st century jobs, you must understand **personal branding.** Yes, we've discussed it before, but let's look at it again; it has special significance for this final chapter of the book.

The term is tossed around a lot and has millions of interpretations. As you can probably guess by now, my view of personal branding relates specifically to being the CEO of ME, Inc. and running your career as a business.

Branding is all about *image* and *perception.* When McDonald's first thought about a logo for their company, they had to choose between a sketch of a hamburger with a bag of fries next to it or a sketch of two golden arches joined together. McDonald's went with the arches. Why? **Because it was memorable.** It became easy for consumers to associate the fast food chain with the golden arches because the McDonald's marketing team knew how customers thought, how they reacted to certain visual stimuli, color preferences, shapes, and so on. *As it turned out, their assessment was dead-on!*

Branding basically asks this question: What is it about *you* that's totally unique — either no one else does it, or no one else does it better than you? When you have that answer, you've got the beginning of a powerful personal brand.

Many marketing experts think of branding as an individual's "trust mark", shorthand, or signature. I like to think of it as a person's *reputation.*

As you develop a personal brand that helps you break away from the pack, it will tell everyone who you are, what you do, how you do it, and what makes you different from everyone else; in other words, how *you* create value and benefit in a way that no one else can.

That's the basic idea of personal branding. The greater challenge, however, is to develop and deploy a **branding strategy** that sets you apart from your competition. For that, dig into some of the literature about branding available at bookstores, on the Internet and in your local library. If your brand is memorable and your strategy is flawless, your ME, Inc. business will flourish.

A final caveat: When you select your brand and brand strategy, make sure they fit like a pair of gloves. Once people see and experience your brand, the worst thing you can do is change or retract it because that can create a perception of instability, about the last image you want projected out into the marketplace.

Finally, do your personal branding homework. You won't regret the time you spend since it's a direct investment in your ME, Inc. enterprise.

12.3   The Power of Differentiation

Close on the heels of personal branding is the need to understand the marketing principle called **differentiation.** For now, think of it as "advanced branding."

When you're in business (and you are), *differentiation* says that **your** product or service stands out because it adds unique value and provides customer benefits that your competitors either can't provide or simply don't provide.

Maybe your company's microchips are blazingly fast and drastically reduce computation time. Maybe your automobile engines consistently deliver 45% better gas mileage. Whatever the perceived value or benefit is, that's what *differentiates* you from your competitors.

Now let's apply the differentiation principle to ME, Inc. and the race for 21st century jobs. Back in Chapter 4 when you assembled your value proposition for a well-targeted position, how much of **yourself** did you put into those documents? Did you engineer any unique features into the documentation that helped to brand you as a creative thinker or problem-solver?

One ETP Network member recently told me about her decision to push the envelope on her targeted resume. She was tired of getting passed over for great opportunities. So she started to give a lot of thought to her personal brand and how she could project her values and unique talents using her targeted resume as a platform.

*Her solution? She designed an eye-catching personal logo and composed a brief but **powerful** tagline that captured her unique talents. She embedded the graphic and tagline into the header of her resume so it appeared prominently on each page. The tagline alone made an unforgettable impression as she accepted an increasing number of invitations for interviews.*

*The lesson? This woman pushed her creative talents **beyond** the edge and came up with something special, something that made a lasting impression on an untold number of decision-makers.*

An older, west coast gentleman who'd spent most of his life in financial management included some informative, appropriately-sized pie charts in his resume to emphasize the impact he'd made at two of his former companies.

Are there rules against including pie charts in resumes? I don't think so. They may not be appropriate in all cases and they certainly won't work for everyone. But this gentleman was creative and gutsy. He hadn't seen resumes that came close to using charts effectively, yet he saw the task as a challenge, planned the layout very carefully, and created some eye-catching and informative graphics.

Assuming that he works this way in other aspects of his career management business, it's a safe bet that he has discovered a reliable way to differentiate himself from his competitors.

Failure to differentiate doesn't necessarily mean you'll lose the race ... but it doesn't position you anywhere near the front of the pack, either.

12.4   Lead, Follow or Get out of the Way

Thomas Paine supposedly coined the expression "Lead, follow, or get out of the way." If he were alive today, I'm sure Mr. Paine would probably get a chuckle out of this story:

In 1992, two airlines became embroiled in a lawsuit because both were using the tagline "Plane Smart." They decided to resolve the matter in an extremely unconventional way: The CEO of Southwest Airlines, Herb Kelleher, accepted a challenge from the CEO of Stevens Aviation to settle their legal dispute with an arm-wrestling match. The plan was simple, bold — and totally outrageous: Whoever won the arm-wrestling match would keep the rights to the tagline!

Kelleher lost the match, but the media attention over the event generated so much good will and public interest in both companies that Stevens agreed to let Southwest use the line.

Was Herb Kelleher an exceptional business leader? **Or was he just plain nuts?** Most business analysts agree that his bold, audacious participation in this event was enough to keep him in the leadership spotlight for a long time.

Clearly, being bold and audacious can work in a CEO's favor, but it can backfire too. By participating in such a high-profile and thoroughly bizarre maneuver, Herb Kelleher took a great risk, the risk of being perceived as a buffoon. But I like to think that the mistakes he made earlier in his career taught him how to use good judgment. Experience probably showed him how to weigh the possible outcomes of certain behaviors — so much so that when he agreed to participate in the arm-wrestling stunt he was actually executing a well-planned strategy.

A CEO doesn't have to be unconventional to be successful, but he or she does need a core set of leadership skills that are considered vital to the organization's success.

Note: The arm-wrestling leadership story about Herb Kelleher is included in a great book called <u>NUTS! Southwest Airlines' Crazy Recipe for Business and Personal Success</u> by Kevin and Jackie Freiberg (Bard Press, Austin, TX).

12.5   Why Leadership?

You've come a long way since reading the Introduction to this book. In my view, that means you are well on your way to winning the race for 21st century jobs. If the book's core messages are genuinely taking root, you're also in the process of creating a well-defined, well-branded and well-differentiated niche in the 21st century jobscape.

That can only mean one thing: It's time for you to "graduate" to a new level of networking and CEO career management proficiency — it's time for you to become a *networking leader.*

Why leadership?

I think of leadership as the rudder by which an organization steers its course to achieve its mission and embody its vision. Take leadership away and the group becomes a rudderless vessel, adrift and directionless. Organizations without competent, effective leadership simply don't survive.

A networking organization like the ETP Network survives because there are individuals who emerge from the general membership and take the next step in their networking evolution, *the step up to becoming a networking leader.*

Leadership brings out an individual's best qualities. Many people need to be thrust into the spotlight to discover the surprising reach of their capabilities. Avoiding the spotlight entirely is not necessarily harmful, but it can easily prevent you from making any meaningful progress in your career path.

When you take on a leadership role, you're effectively saying, "Look, I've mastered the basics. Now I want to give back to the team that sustained me in the hard times. I'm not doing it because I have to, I'm doing it because I want to, because it's the right thing to do for me and for everyone else." *(Read more about "giving back" in Section 12.7.)*

One of the ETP Network's core goals is to have CEOs of ME, Inc. step into positions of leadership when they believe the time is right. The reason is clear: Those who take on leadership positions strengthen the network by opening up new lines of communication and pathways of opportunity to the membership-at-large. By establishing themselves as trusted advocates of the ETP Network philosophy, they reinforce the organization's objectives and become ambassadors of its mission, vision and values. As a result, they learn about their suitability for leadership — and leadership is a **critical attribute** for those who intend to win the race for 21st century jobs.

12.6   Characteristics of Good Leaders

Although there is general agreement about what characteristics are common to all effective leaders, there is no corresponding authoritative "desk reference" that's ever been published

and widely accepted by business leaders. Instead there are hundreds of books on the subject that **attempt** to do so, adding slightly to the overall confusion. The following qualities are cited most often in literature about leadership. Leaders:

- are authentic and not afraid to be themselves
- have a desire to help others
- empower the people around them
- are guided by heart, passion, and compassion
- recognize their mistakes and shortcomings
- exhibit diligence and have a "never give up" attitude
- build enduring relationships
- know exactly where they stand on issues
- refuse to compromise their values when tested or challenged
- have excellent interpersonal skills
- have excellent communications skills
- project confidence
- are flexible
- adapt well to change
- are highly creative
- nurture creativity in others
- focus on achieving results
- understand the importance of occasional failure
- learn from their mistakes then move on
- build teams
- know when to delegate
- have access to people, information and resources to help solve problems and create opportunities
- have a healthy sense of humor
- help to provide strategic direction for the organization they serve
- have the ability to stay positive at all times (Positive Mental Attitude)
- seek counsel and advice when they recognize the need for it
- know how to inspire others

- have total commitment to their position or niche within the group
- are consistently teachable and coachable
- are willing to step aside rather than compromise the integrity of the team
- are motivated by the welfare of the team instead of their own agenda
- are oriented to whatever the team cannot provide through its own efforts

If you're thinking, "Well, that's an interesting list. But I'm not really interested in taking on any leadership roles right now ... I'm kinda busy" ... I encourage you to close the book for a moment and re-read the title very carefully. Has it hit you yet?

You are in a race with millions of others for a finite number of available positions in the global marketplace. It can be very uncomfortable to view the business world in this way, but unfortunately, that is our 21st century reality and we must all learn to deal with it.

Some have likened today's business climate to a some-what cruel version of musical chairs in which **lots** of players don't get seats when the music stops. Borrowing from that theme, I believe those who **will** find a chair will be those who can demonstrate a mastery of business ownership along with a natural flair for leadership.

CEOs are, by definition, leaders. And because not every-one in pursuit of those limited opportunities will adopt this mind-set, the CEOs of ME, Inc. will find themselves solidly positioned at the front of the pack, uniquely situ-ated to grab jobs and opportunities **away** from those who **chose** not to manage their careers wisely but opted instead for the ease, convenience, and short-sightedness of The Black Hole.

12.7 The Importance of Giving Back

Leaders all over the world recognize the importance of giving back to the organizations that put them in power. ETP Network leaders feel the same way and realize that their selfless efforts make a great difference to the organization as a whole.

Investing time in the group as a leader means helping the "next wave" of CEOs to blossom and grow. An earlier group did it for you, correct? And when you were on the receiving end of all that mentoring, I'll bet you were occasionally curious about how those leaders made their way into those positions of leadership.

Giving back to the organization is clearly not an obligation. But most leaders give back because they know that sustaining the new wave of CEOs will have far-reaching benefits for them, too, e.g., expanding their networks, gaining exposure as networking leaders, providing high-powered resume enhancements, and so on.

Think of it this way: If you have kids, you know how important it is to ensure the success and well-being of the next generation. It's just another reminder that things are not always "just *about me*"; sometimes it's necessary to direct attention to a generation that will someday replace you.

It's the natural order of things.

12.8   Summary: Connections, Relationships & Networking — Chapter 2

Chapter 2 was identified as a "core chapter" because of its focus on learning how to connect properly with others, developing relationships (networking), and building what I like to call a "warm trusted network." Here are the most important summary points:

1.   Master the art of small talk and start making connections.
2.   Never forget that solid, effective networking is always built on trust and reciprocity. If you understand and value both, there's no end to the growth of your network.
3.   If a connection is meant to deepen into a trusted relationship, you'll know it soon enough.
4.   Vigorously build and track your network.
5.   Use the *ping principle* to stay in touch with your network.
6.   Learn to *manage* your network *("Seed / Feed / Weed")*.
7.   Networking is smart business.
8.   Protect the connector!
9.   Build your network *before* you need it.

12.9   Summary: The CEO of ME, Inc. Paradigm — Chapter 3

Chapter 3 was identified as a "core chapter" because it presents and explains the concept of being a CEO of ME, Inc. Having a firm grasp on this mind-set is the key determinant of your success with the entire program. Here are the most important summary points:

1. Think, speak, and act like a business owner because you are one.
2. Whatever you finally decide to do, it's *your move*. You assume full responsibility.
3. Take charge of your career not just for yourself, but for your Personal Board of Directors.
4. Visualize the job search process as a group of interconnected departments (e.g., R & D, Sales & Marketing, etc...); this will deliver results more smoothly and efficiently. That's because grouping specific tasks by function allows you to stay fully focused on results, not process.
5. CEOs discipline themselves to get results. Why? Their Board of Directors *demand it*.
6. Adopt mental toughness and a "positive mental attitude" in everything you do as a CEO. Don't just think it — **do it!**

12.10   Summary: The ETP Network Value Proposition — Chapter 4

Chapter 4 was identified as a "core chapter" because it offers the "attraction model" for gaining ground in the race for jobs and contracts. This is where you learn how to "build your case" for a particular job or position. Here are the most important summary points:

1. Be completely familiar with your own skills and talents.
2. Understand what the ETP Network value proposition is: Job Description (for which you are

eminently qualified) / Targeted Resume / T-Letter cover letter.

3. *Own the job description* and you'll develop a rock-solid value proposition that helps you deliver a "clincher" interview. No decision-maker wants to exclude someone with a powerful value proposition, especially when it demonstrates "dead on" relevance.

4. Submit only *targeted resumes (TRs)* for positions you desire and are qualified to pursue. Don't ever submit a generic resume for a position you're interested in.

5. Always develop your targeted resume first; then base your T-Letter on the experience section of your TR going back 3 – 5 years.

6. Learn how to draft convincing, compelling T-Letters that follow the "four L's": *Layout, Logic, Linkage, and Language.*

7. Remember: *Benefits Always Trump Features.* You need to give people motivation if you want them to help you. You need to *sell the benefit.*

8. A top-notch value proposition is the key to getting the interview; the interview is the key to getting the job.

12.11 Summary: The 7-Step Job Search Methodology — Chapter 5

Chapter 5 was identified as a "core chapter" because it is the centerpiece of the entire career management program, i.e., the actual 7-Step Job Search Methodology. Following this methodology consistently increases your potential for reaching the interview stage. Here are the most important summary points:

1. The job search will be a piece of cake as long as your skills are *in demand by the market you're pursuing!!!*
2. On the targeted resume, be sure to give the client what he or she is looking for, not an overblown catalog of your entire business experience.
3. Any employer will hire any individual as long as the employer believes hiring that person will bring more value than it costs (the Universal Hiring Rule).
4. When you connect with advocates (Group A and Group B), remember to follow up. Failure to follow up is one of the biggest reasons why many job searches come to an abrupt halt.
5. The 7-Step Job Search Methodology *improves the probability* of finding a job *but it **does not guarantee** that you'll find a job.*

12.12   What and Where is the Finish Line?

Let's talk about the finish line for a moment.

If you're envisioning a hyperventilating, sweat-soaked, spandex-clad runner smashing through a red ribbon with clenched fists high in the air and a look of jubilation on her face, forget it. Wrong kind of race.

There are two ways to view the finish line in the race for 21st century jobs. Both are natural by-products of the conceptual and procedural job search framework I've built within this book. They represent the ETP Network's "dual view" of the finish line, one abstract and the other practical.

The Abstract View of the Finish Line

Most of you have already figured out that there is no such thing as a "finish line" in the race for 21st century jobs. How **can** there be? What **is** there that can ever possibly be "finished"? The work involved to position yourself as a uniquely qualified candidate never ends, not even after you've land a targeted position.

It's safer to think of the race for 21st century jobs as a race with an unlimited number of competitors and no discernible end, no finish line. As you've seen in this book, the real work of keeping yourself competitive never ends.

The Practical View of the Finish Line

You've reached a **kind** of finish line when you can answer the following questions with an unqualified **Yes!** *and when the enthusiasm behind that* **Yes!** is driven by an undiluted commitment to both your ME, Inc. business and your Board of Directors:

- Are you free and clear of The Black Hole? Are you sure?
- Do you have solid "small talk" skills?
- Do you have solid "connecting" skills?
- Do you have solid "relationship-building" skills?
- Do you understand the importance of "protecting the connector"?
- Do you understand the importance of network maintenance?
- Are you constantly expanding your network, either while in transition or while employed?
- Are you comfortable in the role of CEO of ME, Inc.?
- Do you fully understand what we mean by the *value proposition?*

- Do you have a "Ph.D." in reading and interpreting job descriptions?
- Are you adept at drafting effective targeted resumes?
- Are you adept at drafting effective T-Letters?
- Do you understand the phrase "sell the benefit"?
- Do you fully understand the 7-Step Job Search Methodology?
- Are you someone who understands the value and necessity of having Group A and Group B advocates?
- Do you consistently follow up, using the appropriate communications medium?
- Are you up to speed with online tools such as *LinkedIn* and *Indeed?*
- Do you recognize the raw potential of *The Hidden Job Market?*
- Do you understand why we say that your job search begins once you've accepted a position?
- Are you up to speed on all aspects of social networking and social media?
- Are you aware of leadership qualities and the importance of being a networking leader?
- Do you understand and use personal branding?
- Do you have a personal brand of your own?
- Do you understand the power of differentiation?
- Are you up to speed on current trends in business and technology?
- Have you read this book cover-to-cover?
- Have you joined the ETP Network?
- Do you believe you have the capacity to run your career as a business?

There are several more bullets I could add to this list, but from my perspective, an affirmative response to them constitutes a major victory.

12.13   Because It's the Right Thing to Do

In reaching the end of this book, you've really reached a new beginning. You know what the challenges are and how to sidestep the most damaging obstacles. Now you need to plot a course of action that will consistently help you to land the next interview, job or client.

It begins with that first bold decision to abandon The Black Hole once and for all. The jobs of the 21st century are an entirely different breed from those in the past and if you're not in the "pack" already, you need to establish a comfortable starting point within it *now.* Joining the ETP Network will be a critically important step in the right direction because of the support it offers.

I am quite confident that you will give the ETP Network a close look. And I'm convinced that if you give us a try — at least for a short-term engagement — you'll find a pathway to your next position that's practically lit up with runway lights. You may scratch your head wondering why you lounged around in The Black Hole for so long. And best of all, an entire community of fellow ETP Network members will be there to support you every step of the way — not to mention the millions you'll connect with on *LinkedIn!*

As you become increasingly comfortable in the role of CEO of your own business, making critical decisions will become much easier. Possibilities which once seemed out of reach will now appear far more accessible and attainable — and why shouldn't they? Your expert analysis of market conditions (both *spot* and *future*) combined with top-notch business intelligence gives you an incomparable advantage over those who opted for the ease and convenience of The Black Hole.

Is Your Personal Board of Directors Worth It?

The *New Corporate You* understands the huge stakes riding on your performance: Does your Personal Board of Directors actually *prefer* that you spend Sunday afternoons tossing darts at the *Help Wanted* section of the newspaper or hanging out in The Black Hole? Or do they want you fully engaged with a system that practically guarantees an interview every time?

Here's the reason I'm confident you'll get rid of the *Help Wanted* section: **You don't need it any more.** Instead, you'll now dig for opportunities in a logical and systematic way. You'll learn everything you can about each opportunity and earn your Ph.D. in Job Descriptions. From that difficult and often tedious work, you'll undoubtedly pick up a few battle scars here and there, but you'll also end up impressing decision-makers, getting interviews, and most likely landing the kind of positions that are the envy of everyone else in the pack.

I firmly believe that you'll give the ETP Network a try. Why am I so sure? Because you're a rational individual who has already demonstrated an eagerness to try a better **kind** of job search. That's the reason you bought this book, isn't it?

I think you'll check out ETP because I've struck a chord somewhere in your psyche that tells you there is finally a path through the job search wilderness that's logical, systematic, and results-oriented. Yes, it's hard work and yes, it's work that you must shoulder almost entirely by yourself. But within the ETP Network, there are thousands of friends who will help you, guide you, and encourage you every step of the way.

As a matter of fact, I'll go so far as to say that probably none of you who read this book and truly absorb its contents will even consider joining the ETP Network for any of the wrong reasons (to save time, to outsource your workload, to broadcast your entitlement tendencies, etc.).

Instead you will join to **challenge yourself, push yourself, and empower yourself** so that you can be in total control of **all** your career management decisions. You will join for all the right reasons.

Finally and most importantly, I believe you'll join the ETP Network to support the people who matter to you the most: your Personal Board of Directors. You'll do it because they deserve the very best you have to offer. **They are counting on you to win the race for 21st century jobs.**

Own your career — because it's the right thing to do for you, your family and your future.

You have the power to claim victory ... but first you have to be in the race!

Beyond ME, Inc.

- CEOs of ME, Inc.
- Business Leaders
- Strategic Partners

You probably read Chapter 12 and thought the story was over. Quite the contrary: The story is *just beginning.* The race for 21st century jobs doesn't stop just because you've successfully navigated your way into a targeted position or landed that ideal client; this entire program is *much more than simply "landing a job."*

If you've internalized the CEO of ME, Inc. paradigm, you now recognize its unique value as a powerful business strategy, too. Simply put, *you become a business leader within your network not only because it's the right thing to for the network, but because it's the right thing to do for your own business.* There is an obvious mutual benefit in this type of business model.

In my view, there are three levels of CEOs that emerge from applying the principles developed in this book:

1. **CEOs of ME, Inc.**
   Many people will master and implement the job search methodology and CEO mind-set described in this book and go on to find opportunities whenever they're needed. They are winners in the race for 21st century jobs because they've discovered that the process — the ETP Network Job Search Process — really works.

2. **CEOs as Networking Leaders**
   A smaller group will move into positions of leadership, recognizing the value of helping

others while improving their branding, exposure, and ever-expanding networks, all of which nourish their own CEO of ME, Inc. business.

Networking Leaders are winners in the race for 21st century jobs because they see the **long-term potential** of owning their careers and establishing business rules based on reciprocity and trust. They recognize the extraordinary business value in branding themselves as someone who gives freely and without restriction.

3. **CEOs as Strategic Partners**

Finally, there is an elite group of entrepreneurs who combine the CEO of ME, Inc. paradigm with dynamic leadership to develop truly creative and powerful business strategies. Their unique application of the ME, Inc. paradigm is built on tapping the immense reserves of talent and opportunity within their networks to promote products and services that are in high demand. Once the profit motive is appropriately factored in to the business model — while preserving trust, integrity, and the inherent value of relationships — we now have a **strategic partner, the highest level of CEO career and business management.**

Strategic Partners recognize that they can develop a powerful for-profit business that leverages their good works and deeds to provide an array of products and services within a trusted network. They also recognize that the products and services they provide are limitless because the network of consumers is already built and ready to be leveraged.

Aureo Capiral

Aureo has moved into many lines of business from a small staffing firm to global/medical/career management and international businesses.

Shape My Career, LLC

Shape My Career, LLC helps businesses with the outplacement of displaced employees and offers career coaching to individuals. It uses the tools and techniques provided in this book and leverages the power and diversity of the ETP Network in creating an outplacement program that allows it to stay connected with displaced employees long after the sessions are done.

MedTalents, Inc.

MedTalents ,Inc. provides Healthcare staffing services.

TechnoSphere, Inc.

TechnoSphere, Inc. provides staffing services in other areas, with particular concentration in Information Technology and Finance.

The three companies work together to ensure the success of both the candidate and the employer.

Tony Colón

Techno-Logic Solutions, Inc.

Anthony "Tony" Colón has over 20 years of experience as a Sales and Marketing professional including a multifaceted employment background with a track record of success at local, regional, national and international levels. Known as a creative problem solver, he consistently demonstrates an ability to drive revenue growth, resolve conflicts, improve morale, and exceed profit goals.

He left the corporate sector in 1999 and established Techno-Logic Solutions, Inc.to provide consulting services in various disciplines including language, culture and human services. He speaks 3 foreign languages and is a legal and medical Spanish Interpreter. Having relocated to the Mohawk Valley from the NY City area in 1986 he now considers this area his home and resides in South Utica with his family.

Ruth Harenchar

NBT Associates

Before launching her own IT consulting practice as Spire Solutions Group, the pinnacle of Ruth's career was being a Corporate Officer (Senior Vice

President and Chief Information Officer) at a Fortune 1000 company. Now she is a multi-faceted entrepreneur. She is a Managing Partner in NBT Associates, Chief Networking Officer in ETP Network, and a Senior Sales Associate with Pre-Paid Legal Services.

Recognized as a technology leader and quoted in *InformationWeek*, *Optimize*, *NetworkWorld*, *InfoWorld*, *ComputerWeekly*, *CIO Decisions* and elsewhere on a variety of technology and leadership issues, Ruth's real passion is making the world a better place to live. She has served on a number of non-profit boards – most recently as Chairman of Easter Seals New Jersey.

Carl Reid

SavvyIntrapreneur

Carl landed his first managerial position at age 16. He has over 40 years of business experience, including 26 years as an information technology expert and 16 years as a business career coach. He is CEO and Founder of NetTECH Systems Reid & Associates, Inc.. Carl has been a professional blogger and social media expert since 2004. In addition to being a sought after speaker, he publishes Library of Congress recognized newsletter blogs www.SavvyIntrapreneur.com and www.iTechSpeak.com. Carl is Chief Operations Officer for Empowering Today's (ETP) Network. Email: Carl@etpnetwork.com

Phyllis Shelton

iPower Global Solutions

As CEO and founder of iPower Global Solutions, Phyllis' team provides clients with elaborate event productions and public relations services. Clients include Bill and Hillary Clinton, New York Jets, Caribbean Tourism Organization, Local 1199, Tribeca Film Festival and Nike to name a few. Phyllis is a member of Sisters to Sisters International an organization which empowers women of all backgrounds, especially women of African descent. She was nominated to serve as Vice President of the African American Women of Westchester Political Caucus, District Leader for the 4th Congressional District in New Rochelle, New York and is a member of the Board of Advisors New Rochelle Lego League. Phyllis believes in helping others succeed.

Chip Hartman

MeridiaSystems.com, LLC

Co-author and Editor-in-Chief Chip Hartman is the CEO of MeridiaSystems.com, a company specializing in the design and delivery of web-based visual communications targeted for high-impact marketing and advertising projects.

Chip blends his passion for writing, graphics and technology into one cohesive set of services for companies that want to ensure their "message" is not only reaching the target audience but making a powerful impression, as well.

Acknowledgements

I cannot name all the people who have been important in my journey as businessman, author, motivational speaker and career & business coach in the writing of Win the Race for 21st Century Jobs so I'll just say that I have been blessed with numerous role models, mentors, teachers and friends throughout my several careers. In many ways, everything I write has been born of those relationships.

If anyone deserves the lion's share of credit for the creation of this book it is my co-author and ETP Network Editor-in-Chief Chip Hartman. Chip's determination and belief in getting the ETP message out to the global community was critical to the success of the book.

Thank you to Ruth Harenchar, our production supervisor, for managing the enormous tasks in publishing the book. Your wisdom and guidance was essential to its success.

Thank you to Cheryl Jefferson for doing such an outstanding job in editing the book through numerous iterations.

Thank you to Richard Laurent for managing the critical tasks involved in getting the final draft prepared for printing.

Thank you to Nestor Rodriguez for being a special branding muse.

Thank you to Linda Orlando for many years of loyal friendship, substantive support, and experienced executive perspective guidance to me personally and to the ETP Network.

Thank you to Mary Anne Arneel for being the angel numerous times when we needed extra help in some way to keep the manuscript moving forward to publication.

Thank you to Tom Kenny for serving as the ETP Network content consultant.

Thank you to Su Brooks for serving as the ETP Network graphics consultant.

Thank you to Carl Reid for serving as an advisor concerning all aspects of the ETP Network's programs and operations.

Thank you to the investment team who had the faith in a message that will help to improve the lives of people all over the world.

Thank you to my Personal Board of Directors, Maria, Rod III, Nick and Alicia. I do everything for you.

And lastly, thank you God: Your message I serve in a very unique way.

Rod Colón   *Profile*

www.etpnetwork.com

A Fresh Approach to Personal Success

ETP Network Founder and CEO **Rod Colón** has a unique perspective on what it takes to succeed in today's global economy. Rod shares his 24 years of experience as a corporate HR management insider, outside agency recruiter, corporate trainer, professional speaker and career coach through an unusual yet common sense approach to networking and career management. His in-depth knowledge of international staffing, recruiting and networking gives Rod a unique ability to both coach **and** consult today's professionals and executives around the world.

A Genuine Passion for Helping Others

Rod uses his passion, energy, and creativity to support others. He coaches professionals in the art of leveraging relationships that maximize personal networking opportunities. Rod also uses this hands-on approach with corporations as they confront the new business paradigm in which an organization's success requires professionals to optimize their use of both internal and external networks. As he reminds his members, mastering the subtle techniques of using these networks is vital to the success of both the professional and the organization.

Applying the Power of Networking Technologies

Today the ETP Network leads the way in the education
of networking as a core career management activity
through networking events, career coaching programs,
conference calls, training seminars, job openings, channel partnering and networking libraries. Rod encour-
ages ETP Network members to share their networking
experiences and questions through various events, programs, and webinars and urges members to become
proficient with social media applications such as
LinkedIn, Twitter, and *Facebook.*

Awards, Honors, and Media Recognition

Rod is a graduate of Georgian Court University
and a board member of the Georgian Court Alumni
Association. He has been featured in Princeton Review,
and has received numerous awards and citations in
both print and online media. His innovations with
the ETP Network have attracted a growing audience
of business professionals who recognize and appreciate
his gift for leadership, his command of both traditional
and emerging business trends, and his intense desire
to mentor, coach, train and counsel in all matters
related to career management and personal growth.

Running the Business of "ME"

Index